DILWALE DU

ANUPAMA CHOPRA is a film critic, author and director of the Mumbai Film Festival. She is also the film critic for *Hindustan Times* and founder and editor of the digital platform Film Companion which offers a curated look at cinema.

She has written about the Hindi film industry since 1993 and has explored cinema in several mediums – print, television and digital. From 2012 to 2014, she anchored *The Front Row* on Star World. Her work has been published extensively in *India Today* and she has also written about Bollywood for various international publications such as the *New York Times*, the *Los Angeles Times*, *Variety* and *Sight & Sound*. She is currently a contributing editor to *Vogue* (India). She has written several books on cinema, including *The Front Row: Conversations on Cinema*, *100 Films to See Before You Die*, *Freeze Frame*, *First Day First Show: Writings from the Bollywood Trenches*. Anupama has also written a biography of Shah Rukh Khan titled *King of Bollywood: Shah Rukh Khan and the Seductive World of Indian Cinema*. Her first book, *Sholay: The Making of a Classic*, won the prestigious National Award (given by the President of India) for the Best Book on Cinema.

DILWALE DULHANIA LE JAYENGE

A Modern Classic

ANUPAMA CHOPRA

HarperCollins *Publishers* India

First published in 2002 by the British Film Institute

This edition published in 2016 by
HarperCollins *Publishers* India

Copyright © Anupama Chopra 2016

PISBN: 978-93-5264-100-0
EISBN: 978-93-5264-101-7

2 4 6 8 10 9 7 5 3 1

Anupama Chopra asserts the moral right to be identified
as the author of this work.

The views and opinions expressed in this book are the author's own
and the facts are as reported by her, and the publishers are not in
any way liable for the same.

All rights reserved.
No part of this publication may be reproduced,
stored in a retrieval system, or transmitted, in any form or by any
means, electronic, mechanical, photocopying, recording or otherwise,
without the prior permission of the publishers.

HarperCollins *Publishers*
A-75, Sector 57, Noida, Uttar Pradesh 201301, India
1 London Bridge Street, London, SE1 9GF, United Kingdom
Hazelton Lanes, 55 Avenue Road, Suite 2900, Toronto, Ontario M5R 3L2
and 1995 Markham Road, Scarborough, Ontario M1B 5M8, Canada
25 Ryde Road, Pymble, Sydney, NSW 2073, Australia
195 Broadway, New York, NY 10007, USA

Typeset in 11/15.2 Adobe Garamond
Jojy Philip New Delhi 110 015

Printed and bound at
Thomson Press (India) Ltd.

For Vinod
Tujhe dekha to yeh jana sanam

Contents

Introduction to the New Edition   ix
Acknowledgements   xiii

1 *Terah ka Tees*: The *DDLJ* Phenomenon   1
2 The Making of a Director   16
3 The Making of a Blockbuster   32
4 Believable Fantasies   68
5 'Come ... Fall in Love'   78
6 Tradition and Modernity, Fear and Comfort   113

Notes   122
Credits   132

Introduction to the New Edition

Anupama Chopra

On a damp day in July, I decided to revisit *Dilwale Dulhania Le Jayenge*. The longest-running film in the history of Indian cinema was still running at Maratha Mandir theatre in Mumbai. In the years since its release on 20 October 1995, *DDLJ* had attained a mythical status. The film didn't adhere to any known cinematic rules – it still seduced viewers. It continued to be relevant – directors were still referencing it and paying homage. And it still dominated the cultural conversation: on 27 January 2015, US President Barack Obama stood at the Siri Fort Auditorium and explained why they had not scheduled any dancing on this visit by quoting a dialogue from *DDLJ*. The President said, 'Senorita, *bade bade deshon mein* ... you know what I mean.'

In February 2015, after a record-breaking 1009-week run, the producers Yash Raj Films decided that the film was finally done. But the announcement that *DDLJ*, available everywhere on DVD, would be pulled from the theatre led to such an outcry that the plan was immediately cancelled. The afternoon and evening screenings at Maratha Mandir are new releases but the 11.30 a.m. show continues to be *DDLJ*.

I had not seen the film on a big screen for more than a decade. So much had changed since I came here in 2002 to interview Kundan, the black market boss, for this book. In the years since, Hindi cinema had evolved into a many-splendoured thing. Hindi films no longer adhered to the template of a three-hour-long melodrama punctuated by comedy, action, song and dance. A generation of new directors, writers and actors had refashioned the mainstream idiom. Hindi films could be song-less, star-less, shorter. Dark, twisted narratives barely raised eyebrows. Dysfunctional urban families were routine. Sex onscreen was casual and ubiquitous.

How, I wondered, would the chaste love story of Raj and Simran still hold. After all, this was a couple that famously spends a night together but they don't even kiss because Raj knows 'what honour means for the Hindustani woman'. This world of virginal non-resident Indians in London and forever smiling, singing, loving families in Punjab, just seemed a little silly now.

But it was also irresistible. The balcony was almost full. The audience was almost entirely men. *DDLJ* had been showing now for more than twenty years but each beat brought cheering and applause – Simran's innocent longing for someone to love, Raj's entry on the football field, Thakur Baldev Singh relenting to a month-long Eurail holiday. The hall erupted with applause when Raj and Simran reunited in the sarson ka khet. Jatin–Lalit's signature tune played in the background and I fell for it all over again.

I was older, a smidgen wiser, a little more cine-literate. I could see the outsized loopholes in logic. (How exactly, in those pre-Google, pre-mobile days, did Raj find Simran in Punjab?) I could see the problematic gender politics. I had analysed the film enough times to know exactly how writer and director Aditya Chopra was pushing our emotional buttons and playing us, as Alfred Hitchcock put it, 'like an organ'.

But, ultimately, none of it mattered. The fantasy Aditya created is so persuasive that it forces you to surrender. After all these years, watching *DDLJ* feels like eating '*ma ke haath ka khana*'. The film now functions as cinematic comfort food. In a world grown increasingly ugly, *DDLJ* provides solace and a smile.

I walked out of Maratha Mandir with a little more exuberance. The rest is dross.

Acknowledgements

The cast and crew, distributors and exhibitors of *DDLJ* who took time out to participate in extensive interviews: Aditya Chopra, who finally broke his silence, Yash, Pamela and Uday Chopra, Shah Rukh Khan, Kajol, Amrish Puri, Farida Jalal, Anupam Kher, Parmeet Sethi, Jatin–Lalit, Manmohan Singh, Honey Irani, Javed Siddiqui, Saroj Khan, Farah Khan, Manish Malhotra, Sharmishtha Roy, Anil Thadani, Harish Dayani, Karan Johar, Rahul Nanda, Shiraz Jiwani, Avtar Panesar, Jawahar Sharma and Kundan, the black marketeer.

For their insights: Dharmesh Darshan, Javed Akhtar, Anjum Rajabali, Mait M. Rao, Dr Murali Desai, Rohan Sippy, Shailaja Bajpai, Komal Nahta.

For their help in research: Jitendra Kothari, Ishara Bhasi in the UK, Shailja Dhar in the USA and Pradeep at the *India Today* Library.

For his patient guidance: Vikram Chandra.

One

Terah ka Tees
The *DDLJ* Phenomenon

'*Terah ka tees, terah ka tees, terah ka tees,*' the black marketeers are muttering under their breath. On a humid Sunday morning at the Maratha Mandir theatre in Mumbai, their business is to make sure that no one goes away disappointed. A blackboard on the balcony ticket window announces: 'This show is sold out'. But the black marketeers repeat their patter urgently: the thirteen-rupee ticket is still available, for only thirty rupees. When a customer bites, they shuffle into a corner to conduct business. Five of them, holding ten tickets each, work the crowd under the shifty gaze of their boss, Kundan. He's been in the trade for three decades and knows every move.

The Maratha Mandir cinema hall, inaugurated on 16 October 1958, has a thousand seats. It is located in a predominantly Muslim area in south-central Mumbai, where towering modern buildings stand next to ramshackle shops and mills. That scalpers are plying their trade here isn't surprising. In a movie-mad country, where around 11,962[1] cinemas satisfy the viewing appetites of twelve million people daily,[2] scalpers aren't just the norm, they are a necessity. One way the film industry gauges the success of a film is by what the black market prices tickets at – for movies with big star cast, a 100-rupee ticket can sell for ten times as much.[3]

What's surprising is that the black marketeers are still doing business for this movie. A film's black market, much like hype, deflates rapidly in the weeks after its release, sometimes within days. The more successful films might have black marketeers doing business for a few months. But *Dilwale Dulhania Le Jayenge (The Brave-hearted Will Take the Bride)* has been running continuously in theatres for more than six years. 'It's a first-grade picture,' Kundan says with the jaded expertise of a man who has seen a thousand films fail, 'that's why the public still comes.'

Dilwale Dulhania Le Jayenge, universally known as *DDLJ,* is the longest-running film in the history of Indian cinema. Since its release on 20 October 1995, the film has run in hundreds of theatres in India and abroad. It has been telecast twelve times[4] and is available in video, VCD and DVD versions. But fans still throng to the theatre. Almost every week a new Hindi film is released,[5] but the audience faithfully flocks back to *DDLJ,* to partake in this familiar pleasure.

Watching *DDLJ* at Maratha Mandir is like participating in communal karaoke, or a performance of a well-known mythological play in a village square. As the story unfolds, the audience cheers, mouths dialogue, and sings along. It is unlikely that anyone is seeing it for the first time. In fact, some people may have seen it fifteen, twenty, even thirty times. Kundan says that they come 'to do time-pass', pass their time in an inexpensive,[6] air-conditioned, entertaining way. He talks of regulars who come every day. 'I've never seen such a craze for a film.'

In 2001, *DDLJ* broke the continuous-exhibition record of *Sholay* (*Embers,* 1975), the film industry's previous benchmark, which had run continuously in a Mumbai theatre called Minerva for five years. In its long run at the box office, *DDLJ* has sold an estimated twenty-five million copies of its soundtrack. HMV, *DDLJ*'s music company, pegs official sales at twelve million tapes; and at least the same amount or more pirated cassettes have been sold. HMV's executive director Harish Dayani estimates that one out of three households in India owns the *DDLJ* soundtrack. And while revenue figures in the Hindi film industry are notoriously unreliable, *DDLJ* is estimated to have done a business of approximately 600 million rupees, making it one of the biggest hits ever.[7] *DDLJ* 'regulars' saunter in even half an hour late for the movie, and leave after their favourite scene or song is over. The pleasure is no longer in the tale itself, but in the telling of it.

DDLJ is a romantic musical, which in itself does not distinguish it from the hundreds of films churned out in India. India is the world's largest producer of films, making around 800 films annually.[8] Of these, the largest number, 200-odd, come from Mumbai.[9] The Bombay film industry – or Bollywood as it is popularly known – is the centre of Hindi film. Bollywood makes a variety of spectacles, ranging from big-budget, multi-star movies to C-grade quickies made on threadbare budgets in ten to fifteen days. At any given time, over 250 films are in production and almost each one is both a love story and a musical.

These are the cardinal rules of Bollywood cinema. Whether the film is an action thriller, a war epic, a teen romance or a horror shocker, characters will eventually fall in love and break into a song. Historians believe that this musical form comes from Indian theatre: from the high classical traditions, Parsi theatre and the nautanki or street theatre. A Hindi film without songs is automatically classified as art-house fare, and considered box office suicide. Film songs, which are played at weddings, festivals, parties and nightclubs, are national anthems. They can often make the difference between hit and flop.

The Bollywood film relentlessly mixes genres and styles. Abrupt shifts in location, logic, tone and temper are natural, and in keeping with the skilled mixing of bhavas or shifting emotional states that the classical Indian aestheticians advised. When the warbling hero shifts mid-song from Mumbai to Gstaad, the viewer is unfazed. The emphasis isn't on realism – in the Western sense of the word –

but on spectacle. Each film blends varying degrees of romance, drama, comedy, action and music to create a distinctive masala mix. It will also have enough plot twists to keep a viewer in the seat for three hours.[10]

More than anything, the Bollywood film is a balancing act. Sociologist Ashis Nandy writes:

> Popular film ideally has to have everything – from the classical to the folk, from the sublime to the ridiculous and from the terribly modern to the incorrigibly traditional ... An average 'normal', Bombay film has to be, to the extent possible, everything to everyone. It has to cut across the myriad ethnicities and lifestyles of India and even of the world that impinges on India.[11]

The Bollywood film director aims to equally engross both the villager in Bihar and the second-generation American-born Indian in Boston. This is a near-impossible task.[12]

DDLJ managed it. The film's story is simple. Raj Malhotra, twenty-something, is a wealthy, second-generation British Asian. Born and raised in London, he is flamboyant, irreverent and a relentless flirt. But underneath the cling film of cockiness, he is an essentially good-hearted and moral Indian. Simran Singh, eighteen, is a spirited but traditional middle-class girl brought up in Southall. Raj's father is a robust, back-slapping millionaire. Simran's is a stern, patriarchal convenience-store owner. Raj and Simran, opposites in every way, go for a month-long trip on the Eurail with their respective friends. At first they fight, but eventually – over missed trains, faulty car engines and one cold, drunk night in Switzerland – they fall in love. The hitch is that Simran is already engaged. She was betrothed to Kuljeet, her father's best friend's son in Punjab, when she was a little girl. Soon she will move to a country she has never even visited, to marry a man she has never met.

When Chaudhry Baldev Singh, Simran's father, overhears her confessing her love to her mother, he sells his business overnight and ships his family back to Punjab. Simran's marriage is set to take place in a few weeks. Baldev believes that he has the situation under control, but he doesn't count on Raj's tenaciousness. Raj follows Simran to Punjab. But unlike lovers in countless Bollywood romances, he doesn't elope with her. Instead he stays in the village under a false identity and endears himself to her family. Eventually, after many tears and some blood have been shed, Raj even wins over Baldev. Despite the odds, Raj is always confident that one day he will marry Simran with her father's consent because, as the title promises us, the brave-hearted will take the bride.

When debutant director Aditya Chopra, then barely twenty-three, was writing the story on foolscap sheets in longhand, he hardly imagined that he was creating history. *DDLJ* bent Hindi film convention out of shape and gave it a modern sensibility. Aditya fulfilled Bollywood's myriad requirements, but expertly orchestrated the rhythms to create a fresh and invigorating movie experience. *DDLJ* became a trendsetter, spawning an avalanche of imitations. Directors mimicked its story and manoeuvres through the 1990s, until the *DDLJ* style eventually became a cliché itself.

With *DDLJ*, the expatriate national, the NRI or non-resident Indian, took centre stage. For decades, Hindi film directors have been fascinated by things foreign. Raj Kapoor's *Sangam* (*Union*, 1964) was among the early films to be shot abroad.[13] Aditya's father, film-maker Yash Chopra, was one of the pioneers in popularizing foreign locations. He shot parts of *Silsila* (*The Affair*, 1981) in the tulip gardens of Holland, and then with *Faasle* (*Distances*, 1985) shifted his sights to Switzerland. Yash shot in Switzerland so often that the government recognized him as an official guest.[14] But Yash, like other filmmakers, used foreign locations mostly as a gorgeous song backdrop.[15] Characters would be suddenly transported abroad for love and lip-sync, and then the story would resume in India.

The NRI hardly featured. When he did make an appearance, it was as a debauchee who did all the things upright Indians weren't supposed to, namely, drink, smoke, gamble and lust. In these films, the West was as dangerous as any Orientalist's East – seductive but spiritually fatal. One of the earliest films to portray the Indian diaspora was *Purab aur Paschim* (*East and West*, 1970). The protagonist, Bharat (also a name for India in Hindi), the son of a dead freedom fighter, goes to London for further studies. Bharat doesn't smoke, drink or gamble, and is so respectful that he addresses even the butler with the honorific 'ji'.

The West is represented by an assortment of unsavoury characters who have bottle-blond hair, shortened names (the villain, a lecherous gambler, calls himself OP), and no moral mooring. The NRI children are confused and misled. The son is a hippie, and the daughter a nightclubbing tart who wears miniskirts, drinks and blows smoke rings defiantly into the camera. But Bharat transforms them both into respectful, traditional, fully clad citizens. So much so that the whole family eventually abandons the materialistic glitter of the West for the simpler but superior pleasures of India. The last shots show the daughter emptying a whisky bottle into the drain while the mother tears up the return tickets to London.

DDLJ turned Bollywood's NRI stereotype on its head. The film's protagonists weren't Indians temporarily placed abroad by plot or song but second-generation NRIs. And despite being born and raised in London, both Raj and Simran are unfailingly moral. Their clothes might be trendy (Raj practically lives in a Harley-Davidson leather jacket and jeans), but their value system is traditional Indian. In fact, *DDLJ* did away with the westernized baddie. The most reprehensible character in the film, Simran's chauvinistic and lecherous fiancé, is a thoroughbred Punjabi.[16] It also used foreign locales as part of the storytelling rather than as wallpaper for songs.

DDLJ altered film romance. In 1994, another young director, Sooraj Barjatya, had created box office history with *Hum Aapke Hain Koun…?* (*Who Am I to You?*).[17] The film centred around a wedding and was essentially a celebration of the undivided Hindu family. *DDLJ*, coming a year later, reaffirmed the family and the importance of sacrificing individual desire for the larger good. Rebellion and romance were no longer synonymous. These films celebrated love, but with family approval. And the family didn't mean just parents but extended to aunts, uncles, cousins, grandparents, and even the house help and pets.

The trendy yet traditional, which balanced flashy sets and designer clothes with family values, brought the audience back in a new configuration. The 1980s were the nadir for Hindi movies. With the advent of colour television broadcasts in 1982, and the coming of the VCR, the middle classes opted to get their entertainment at home. Cinemas, mostly frequented by lower-class men, crumbled into decrepitude. Film-makers sought to entice their dwindling audiences with higher doses of violence and sex, and so the families found even less reason to come back to the theatres.

Hum Aapke Hain Koun...? rewrote the business. Its producers held back the film from a simultaneous release on video as a hedge against the inevitable piracy. *Hum Aapke Hain Koun...?* was released in limited theatres with hiked-up ticket prices,[18] which further piqued audience curiosity. Besides, with reams of footage devoted to smiling families and traditional Hindu rituals, *Hum Aapke Hain Koun...?* was one film the family could watch together without embarrassment. The middle class returned in droves. So did the youth. *DDLJ*, equally sanitized, confirmed that *Hum Aapke Hain Koun...?* wasn't a random shot. Cinema halls, by one estimate, witnessed a 40 per cent boom in attendance.[19]

The 1995 National Readership Survey reported that the number of people who go to the theatre more than once a week more than doubled from 3 per cent in 1990 to 7 per cent in 1995. *Hum Aapke Hain Koun...?* had set the precedent for hiking up ticket prices; *DDLJ* followed suit, raising prices to as much as 150 rupees in select theatres. The box office was booming. Komal Nahta, the editor of a trade journal called *Film Information,* estimated that from 1994 to 1995, Hindi film business had increased by over 300 per cent.[20]

Pundits believed that young people constituted a major chunk of this business, especially in the urban centres.[21] A veteran Mumbai-based distributor Ramesh Sippy estimated that almost 60 per cent of the audience comprised young people as compared to 30 per cent in the 1980s.[22] Hindi movies were no longer infra dig. The trendy school and college crowd, which once swore by Hollywood, was identifying with a new generation of heroes such as Shah Rukh Khan, Salman Khan and Aamir Khan.

DDLJ helped to widen Bollywood's overseas market. Hindi films have a vast audience outside of India, made up mostly of the twenty million Indian expatriates. Bollywood's overseas business is divided into four main markets – the United States and Canada, the United Kingdom and Europe, the Gulf states, and smaller markets like Fiji, South Africa, Singapore and Sri Lanka. *DDLJ* did business of more than five million dollars worldwide, becoming one of the biggest overseas hits ever. The Indian diaspora couldn't get enough of it. The first generation of NRIs identified with Chaudhry

Baldev Singh, the stern father who pines for his motherland, while their children saw themselves in Raj and Simran. *DDLJ* captured, albeit through rose-tinted glasses, their life and conflicts.

In San Francisco's Naz theatre, 11,000 people saw the film in the first week alone. On the first day, 1,000 people showed up to fill 720 seats. The proprietor Shiraz Jiwani had no choice but to run a second show at 1 a.m. and 680 people stayed on for it. For three weeks, Shiraz ran shows around the clock, starting the first at 5 a.m. Even the crack-of-dawn show attracted viewers. Shiraz eventually collected approximately 200,000 dollars from the movie. In the UK, *DDLJ* ran for over a year, collecting 2.5 million pounds. Though tickets were steep at £10, the halls were packed. Even repeat runs of the film managed to attract decent crowds.

DDLJ's success helped establish the overseas territory as a major market for the Bollywood film-maker. In the 1980s, an A-grade film with well-known stars would sell for 1.5–2 million rupees. A decade later, prices for the overseas rights were up to 90–100 million rupees.[23] Bollywood directors started designing films targeted specifically at the urban Indian and NRI market – romantic stories with stars, vibrant music, slick production values and minimal action. In 1997, at the insistence of Aditya, Yash Chopra opened a distribution office in the UK. In 1998, their US office opened with *Kuch Kuch Hota Hai* (*Something Happens*), directed by Karan Johar, Aditya's close friend and assistant on *DDLJ*, which broke *DDLJ*'s record and grossed over seven million dollars worldwide.

DDLJ was endlessly imitated in both cinema and television. But none of the clones could copy its success. On 29 March 2002, hoardings across India proclaimed the release of a romance called *Kitne Door, Kitne Paas* (*How Distant, How Close*), about two American NRIs, who return to India to marry fiancées they have never met. Critics tore into it as yet another *DDLJ* rip-off, and the audience turned up its nose. Meanwhile, *DDLJ* celebrated 337 weeks of steady revenues. Kundan, the black marketeer, did brisk business and proclaimed confidently, 'This film will run for six more years.'

Two

The Making of a Director

Until he was eight years old, Aditya Chopra believed that everyone in the world made movies. This was hardly his fault. His house in suburban Mumbai was an adda or hang-out for writers, directors and actors. Famous faces like superstar Amitabh Bachchan, writer Javed Akhtar and lyricist Sahir Ludhianvi were evening guests at the Chopra home. Their children – Abhishek Bachchan and Farhan and Zoya Akhtar – were Aditya's playmates. Pamela, Aditya's mother, would often keep the kids busy with a story game. One person would start a story, which the next continued. Farhan's screwball ideas usually earned him a beating from the other kids.[24]

Aditya grew up stubborn, focused and extremely competitive. He sometimes stammered and was uncomfortable with strangers, but, by nine, he was already developing stories. At the mahurat or ceremonial first shot of *Silsila* in 1980, Aditya narrated a script to actress Shabana Azmi. It was the story of a criminal who, after a bout of amnesia, becomes a police officer and is then assigned to investigate a murder he has committed himself. Shabana, a leading name in the emerging Hindi art-house cinema, had a reputation as a formidable performer and intellectual. But Aditya wasn't fazed. He narrated his story with such clarity and confidence that later Shabana told Javed Akhtar that this kid would one day become a major director.

His father had already paved the way. Yash was a Hindi film colossus. He had been at the top of his profession for over forty years. While other filmmakers of his generation sputtered out long ago, Yash continued to make successful films. He was Bollywood's only working director to have delivered a hit in each of the last five decades. Yash's name on the marquee meant good music, beautiful costumes, exotic foreign locations and romance. His romantic style has become a hallmark. As Rachel Dwyer writes, 'His name has come to represent a certain style, not only in film-making but in Indian culture itself, where [it] is synonymous with romance, glamour and beauty.'[25] With a series of hits through the 1990s, the Yash Raj banner has established itself as a Bollywood powerhouse. It encompasses a production house, distribution offices in India and abroad and a state-of-the-art film studio under construction in suburban Mumbai.

Yash came to Mumbai on 1 January 1951, with 200 rupees in his pocket. He was nineteen years old. He came from Lahore, where he was born, to live and work with his elder brother B.R. Chopra. BR had started his career as a film journalist, but he migrated from Lahore to Mumbai in August 1947, just before Partition, and set himself up as an independent film-maker. Yash joined him as an assistant, at 150 rupees per month. For seven years, Yash learned the ropes as a mid-level assistant – he was never the clapper boy, nor the chief assistant. In 1959, BR gave Yash a break as a director with *Dhool ka Phool* (*Blossom of the Dust*). The film was a big success and Yash, only twenty-seven, wondered, 'God has given me so much, but is it temporary or will it go further?'

Yash couldn't possibly conceive how far his career would go. After *Dhool ka Phool,* Yash and BR made films alternately. Among Yash's biggest successes was *Waqt* (*Time,* 1965). *Waqt,* generally acknowledged as Bollywood's first multi-star vehicle, was the beginning of the 'Yash Chopra' style. It depicted a lifestyle rarely seen on screen before – *Waqt*'s two leading ladies, Sadhana and Sharmila Tagore, dressed in the latest fashions, flitted in and out of splendid parties and homes. Two of its three heroes raced foreign cars and played billiards. And many of the characters lived in mansions with fountains bubbling in living rooms. In 1971, a year after his marriage, Yash broke away from BR and founded Yash Raj Films. The banner had several successes, but in the 1980s, when Aditya and his brother Uday were teenagers, Yash was going through his leanest phase.

The 1980s are widely considered to be the dark ages of Bollywood.[26] The industry, haemorrhaging under the twin onslaughts of video and colour television, was trying to find a formula for success. The Angry Young Man of the 1970s, brought to life by Amitabh Bachchan and writers Salim–Javed, had turned into a lifeless cliché. After a decade of

Bachchan's vigilante fists, music had been relegated to the sidelines. The audience, mostly young men, seemed to prefer action and loud, gaudy melodramas, which film-makers from southern India were churning out. In the confusion, Yash flailed around, trying to regain his rhythm. He made film after film with little success: *Kala Patthar* (*Coal,* 1979), *Silsila, Mashaal* (*The Torch,* 1984), *Faasle* and *Vijay* (*Victory,* 1988). All were met with varying degrees of indifference.

Aditya disliked *Faasle.* He had seen it in a preview. He went to see it again on the first day of release to gauge audience reactions. Indian audiences, unlike Western ones, are vocal in their appreciation of cinema. When they like something, there is applause, whistles and even the occasional showering of coins on the screen. The 'repeat audience', people who see the film more than once, are critical to a film's success. In *Faasle,* there was no reaction. Some people were walking out. But Aditya came home and lied to his father that the audience was enjoying the film. It was the first time he felt the sour taste of a film's failure. But the vagaries of making movies didn't dissuade him from his goal. There was no doubt in his mind that he would be a director.

Through school, Aditya was among the top ten students in class, but he didn't want to go to college. It was, in his mind, a waste of time. When Pamela put her foot down, he enrolled for a commerce degree at the Sydenham College of Commerce and Economics, one of Mumbai's leading institutions. Every morning, he would travel to south Mumbai by train, play football and return home. When his parents offered to send him to the United States for further studies, he refused. He wanted to make Hindi movies, and America would make him lose touch. Finally Pamela relented. She wouldn't allow Aditya to drop out of college, but she allowed him to work.[27]

Aditya started as an assistant on *Chandni* (*Moonlight*, 1989). Yash, after a decade of unsuccessfully chasing commercial success with guesses about audience tastes, had decided to return to what he himself liked best – romance. Aditya's first schedule was an outdoor shoot in Switzerland. Since shooting there was prohibitively expensive, the crew was downsized. Yash took only two assistants – his chief assistant Naresh Malhotra and Aditya. Aditya did everything – continuity, costumes, calling artists. The first time he gave the clap, Aditya was petrified. He learned the clap by heart and gave it correctly. But actor Rishi Kapoor couldn't resist ribbing the rookie. 'Why did you give such a loud clap?' he asked the nervous boy. But Aditya learned fast. After Switzerland, everything else was 'a cakewalk'.

Aditya missed some schedules because of exams, but he sat through the post-production processes, including dubbing and mixing. The family and crew watched the finished film at a preview. The air was thick with nervous anxiety. Yash badly needed a hit. *Chandni* was quintessential Yash – a gossamer romance with beautiful people, rich emotions and melodious songs shot abroad. Some people didn't think much of the love triangle but Aditya loved it. 'Mark my words,' he told his mother, 'this will be a superhit.'

It was. *Chandni* marked the reversal of fortune in Yash's career. Aditya's commercial instincts were clearly kicking in. Sometime between *Faasle* in 1985 and *Vijay* in 1988, Aditya had started to study Hindi commercial cinema, in what he calls his 'director's series'. He would pick a director and watch every film he had made. Aditya watched all of Raj Kapoor, Vijay Anand, Raj Khosla, Manoj

Kumar, Bimal Roy, B.R. Chopra and his father.[28] He tried to analyse the mechanics of success: What made a film great? What made it work? How did the masters push audience buttons?

Studying the past wasn't enough. Every Friday, Aditya would head to the nearest theatre to catch the latest release.[29] Unlike the rest of the industry, he didn't want to see movies in cushy preview theatres but experience them in halls with an audience. He became, in Bollywood parlance, a 'first day, first show' man. From 1989 to 1991, Aditya kept diaries of his film viewing. The diaries first summarized the previous year, listing winners in different areas of excellence, from performance to cinematography – these were Aditya's private awards, his own *Filmfare* trophies or Oscars.

The following pages recorded each film Aditya saw, its first-week collections, the box office result in the following weeks, a box office prediction and the actual box office result. There was also a monthly review, looking at the winners and the overall box office performance (November 1990 had no 'Bests' and was described as 'a disgusting month'). At year-end, Aditya would see how accurate his predictions were. He was right 80 per cent of the time.

These diaries were painstakingly written in longhand, in Sydenham College notebooks. Aditya wasn't a snobbish viewer. He consumed everything Bollywood dished out, from C-grade films like *College Girl* (1991) – his review said it was 'the usual rape and revenge film' – to A-grade star-cast films. Aditya also diligently listened to a popular radio countdown show called *Cibaca Geetmala*. He would make his own list of the top ten film songs and compare it with the show. When the family was travelling, the servants were instructed to store the weekly Bollywood trade magazines and record the show. Uday watched his movie-mad brother and simply shrugged his shoulders. 'I wasn't into it at all.'

Lamhe (*Moments*, 1991) was the first film that Aditya was creatively involved in. *Chandni*'s success gave Yash the confidence to try a tricky subject that he had been nursing for some time: a romance between a middle-aged man and a young girl. To make matters more complicated, the girl is the exact replica of her mother, whom the man once loved passionately but never had a relationship with – *Chandini*'s heroine Sridevi played both roles. Aditya, with his box office instincts honed by years of movie watching, told his father not to make it. He believed that a love triangle involving one man and a mother and her daughter 'could never run in India'.

But Yash persisted and Aditya started to work on how to make the subject more palatable. He suggested making the first woman older than the man. *Lamhe* became Aditya's training ground. He worked in each area, from the dialogue sessions to the music recordings. He also made an unconventional trailer for it, cutting the song *'Kabhi tum kaho'* (Sometimes you say) with shots from the film. Aditya wasn't confident about *Lamhe*'s music – he thought it was too sophisticated – but by the time the film was finished, he loved everything about it. His diary entry reads: 'A landmark film … beautifully made … brilliant dialogues, good music, fantastic cinematography … mind-blowing performances … one of the most boldest [sic] and different films ever made … will be a superhit.'

Lamhe flopped. In the first show itself, Aditya knew the film wasn't working. The film got great reviews but the box office wouldn't budge. *Lamhe* didn't play to full houses even during its first weekend. Yash was deeply depressed by the debacle and Aditya retreated into a shell. The failure of

Lamhe further underlined for him the importance of commercial success. He wasn't convinced by arguments that the film was ahead of its time and the audience couldn't grasp it. For Aditya, the audience is God and can never be wrong. The problem was with the film. He watched it repeatedly on video and finally identified twenty minutes of footage – the post-interval portion, which shows the young girl becoming obsessed with the man, her mother's erstwhile admirer – that should have been deleted. Later, he even suggested to Yash that they excise the part and re-release the film under a different name, to see if it worked. But it was too late.[30]

During a break in the making of *Lamhe,* Yash had agreed to direct a film for an outside producer. Aditya was dead against his father being a director-for-hire. He also had his college final exams, so he decided to sit out on *Parampara* (*Tradition,* 1992). The film was finished in six months. When Aditya first saw the rushes, he 'hated it'. After the trial at the Ketnav preview theatre, the unit returned to Yash's house for a dissection. Aditya didn't mince his words. He said the film had to be cut drastically. Later, he sat in on the edit. Yash cut twenty minutes from the film.[31]

'Adi baba' was slowly becoming a voice at Yash Raj Films. The reserved, unassuming boy had grown up into an opinionated young man. And he wasn't shy about expressing his views. When Aditya came to Yash with the idea of a quickie movie about an obsessive lover, Yash listened. *Darr* (*Fear,* 1993), loosely inspired by the thriller *Dead Calm,* was meant to be a small, dark, song-less thriller with young actors. It was going to be directed by Yash's assistant, Naresh. But actor Rishi Kapoor, who was offered one of the lead roles, suggested to Yash that he direct it himself.

When Yash took over the directorial reins, *Darr* automatically became a big movie. Songs and Switzerland were threaded into the narrative. So was a big star cast – Sunny Deol, Juhi Chawla and Aamir Khan – all suggested by Aditya. Eventually Aamir opted out of playing the psychotic lover and another upcoming actor was pencilled in: Shah Rukh Khan.

Through the making of the film Aditya and Shah Rukh became friends. Yash, Sunny and Juhi were clearly 'seniors', older and more successful players in Bollywood's hierarchy. Shah Rukh, successful but not yet the megawatt star, stuck to Aditya and

Uday, who were both assisting. Shah Rukh and Aditya would come up with wacky ideas and then conspire about how best to convince Yash to use them. 'We became schemers,' says Shah Rukh, 'because you don't tell Yash Chopra how to shoot.' *Darr* was the first film in which Yash incorporated scenes that Aditya suggested. Aditya monitored the dubbing and sat in on the editing. Once again, he also cut the trailer for the film.

The *Darr* theatrical trailer was path-breaking. Unlike most Hindi film trailers, this one had no dialogue or songs from the film. Aditya took music from a central dance sequence, cut in sudden flashes of the film, and ended the preview with a shot of the psychotic Shah Rukh simply screaming. The television promos showed Shah Rukh carving the heroine's name on his chest with a knife. Aditya was clear that the audience must not come in expecting the typical peaches-and-cream Yash Raj romance. *Lamhe*'s failure had taught him that each film needs to be marketed uniquely. The strategy worked. *Darr* was a big success.

After *Darr*, Yash told Aditya, 'Now you make a movie.' But Aditya wasn't so sure. He didn't know if he was ready to shoulder the responsibility. He kept busy thinking up ideas for Yash's next film. Among the many floating in his mind was a love story in which the boy and girl meet on a train. The girl is a conservative Indian brought up in London and the boy is American. Aditya imagined an Indian actress with Tom Cruise. The two have a wonderful time in exotic European locations. Only when it's time to part do they realize that they love each other. Tom would then follow the girl to India and through her, discover its people and culture. The film, in English, would cross over to non-Indian audiences as well. Aditya imagined it would be his fourth or fifth film.

In one of their several brainstorming sessions, Aditya bounced the idea off Yash. He was trying to reshape it as a Hindi film and making it up as he narrated. Halfway through, the girl wants to elope with the boy but he refuses. He tells her that he loves her and will only marry her with the consent of her father. When Aditya said this, something sparked. He knew he had hit upon something. Yash, who preferred love stories with a twist, wasn't so keen. 'It's nice,' he said, 'but it's not for me. Why don't you make it?' Aditya had always thought that he would make his debut with *Mohabbatein* (*Loves,* 2000), a more complex tale involving a music teacher and three sets of lovers.[32] But the idea of lovers who don't elope animated him. He ran into his mother's room and asked her if she had five minutes to spare.

Unlike many Bollywood wives of her generation, Pamela has never taken the back seat in the Chopra house. She and Yash had an arranged marriage when she was twenty-two and he was thirty-eight. Like lovers in many of Yash's films, they first met at a wedding. Pamela was singing Punjabi wedding songs. He noticed her singing. She noticed him because the gossip magazines had been writing that he was currently having an affair with leading actress Hema Malini.

Over the years, Pamela anchored Yash's life both personally and professionally. She created a traditional yet modern Punjabi home for her husband and children. A Hindi movie buff, she also became Yash's bouncing board. She suggested the story of *Kabhi Kabhie* (*Sometimes*, 1976). And Yash made it a point to include her in the music sittings, when tunes and lyrics were thought up and tested. She has also sung songs, especially wedding ones, in many of his films. In *Chandni*, Pamela even sang a song for the heroine. Her opinion carries weight.

Aditya's narration was short. Pamela was unequivocal in her response. She loved the story. It was a wonderful script, she felt, because the second half in India was even better than the first in Europe. His mother's reaction was reassurance enough. Aditya decided to make *DDLJ*.

Three

The Making of a Blockbuster

Aditya Chopra narrates his plots in real screen time. The film runs in his head, frame by frame, and he describes what he sees, for more than three hours – the running time of the film. His passion is evident in his intensity. Sometimes, in the emotional scenes, his stammer worsens. But his energy doesn't flag. For *DDLJ*, he started something like this: 'London. Pigeons fluttering across a grey overcast sky, the camera tracks down and you see a man dressed in a traditional Indian dress feeding the birds. Slowly a song starts …'

But Aditya's ardour failed to enthuse the Yash Raj Films unit. Yash's company follows certain traditions. One is that before a new film starts, the top crew is called home and given a detailed narration. In May 1994, cinematographer Manmohan Singh, art director Sharmishtha Roy, dialogue writer Javed Siddiqui and family friend Deven Varma gathered in the Chopras' gadda room (cushion room) to hear what Aditya had in mind. They weren't impressed.

Manmohan didn't like the first half. Plotwise, little happened. Others thought there wasn't enough intensity in the story – why does the boy follow the girl to India when he doesn't even know if she loves him. The climax sounded too much like another successful film, *Dil Hai Ki Manta Nahin* (*The Heart Does Not Listen*, 1991), in which the father encourages his daughter to run away from her own wedding and marry another man. Aditya was devastated. He loved his story. He thought it was brilliant. He asked himself two questions: 'Do you love this script? Will you be a film-maker who speaks his voice?' The answer to both questions was a resounding 'Yes'. Aditya decided to make *DDLJ* as he saw it.

The film was clear in his head. Aditya had never planned to write the film, but only create an outline before going to a writer. The story and characters had come in a rush. Sitting in his bedroom, at a long desk, which he and Uday shared, Aditya started working on an outline, writing in longhand. A few years ago, he had studied at the same desk for his school exams. Sometimes he sat on the lawn. When Aditya was unsure of a scene or when he was too sure, he would use Pamela or Uday as bouncing boards. He also had story sessions with family friend and writer, Honey Irani. His writing was messy but legible. Aditya had the outline in twelve days.

Input also came from an unexpected quarter – Karan, the twenty-two-year-old son of veteran producer Yash Johar. Karan and Aditya had known each other when they were children, but had since lost touch. Their parents were friends and colleagues. But Karan, more posh and resolutely snotty, didn't like the Chopra brothers. 'They spoke in Hindi about Hindi films and I was like, "Please ... how tacky."'[33] But a common college friend, Anil Thadani, whose family was in film distribution, connected them again.

Karan was a closet Bollywood buff. He had devoured the films of all the great Hindi movie directors and tracked box office collections since childhood. But he had never considered a career in films. Instead, he had made vague plans of going to Paris for French studies. But Aditya spotted in Karan a sensibility for popular Hindi films. He encouraged it. Karan thought Aditya's idea for his first film was fantastic. When Aditya started *DDLJ*, he asked Yash for two assistants – Karan and Uday.

Like Karan, Uday was also in denial. He had grown up nurturing a secret dream: he wanted to be an actor in Hindi films, but he couldn't bring himself to admit it.[34] Instead, he went to Los Angeles to do a five-week summer course in filmmaking at the University of Southern California. After that, he had plans to go to Boston to study business management. Like Aditya, Uday had also assisted Yash on *Lamhe* and *Darr* but his heart wasn't in it. He found assisting a chore and couldn't wait till pack-up was announced. Uday had loved the *DDLJ* idea. He wasn't sure why Aditya wanted him, but when Aditya called him in America, he was sure that he should be there. So he went back home after doing a little shopping.

Aditya asked Uday to bring him a leather jacket. He wanted a jacket that radiated modern, cutting-edge 'cool', perhaps with an American flag or an eagle on it. His hero, Raj, would wear it throughout the film. Uday went to a Harley-Davidson store in Bakersfield, California, and picked up a plain black jacket for $400. He then joined Yash in London, where he was scouting for locations in Southall.[35] When he got back to Mumbai, he noticed a change in Aditya – there was now a sudden gravitas. 'I felt the difference between us was no longer a year and a half but six or seven years. He was much older than I was. Much much older.'

Aditya was a director-in-waiting. The last few months had been a flurry of activity. The film's casting was falling into place. Originally Aditya had planned to take newcomers, but as the script took shape, he realized that the film required seasoned performers. Kajol, an actress from a three-generation family of actors, was his first choice for Simran.[36] Aditya had loved her in her debut film *Bekhudi* (*Intoxication,* 1992). With a dusky complexion and hazel-green eyes, she didn't fit the fair-skinned stereotype of the Bollywood heroine. But on screen, she had the charisma of the great screen idols, a mesmerizing intensity from which it was hard to take one's eyes off. Besides, Kajol had worked in a Yash Raj production, *Yeh Dillagi* (*These Love Games,*

1994), and was a friend. Kajol agreed immediately, but wondered how she would play this traditional, obedient daughter. Headstrong and forthright herself, Kajol couldn't relate to Simran at all.

Shah Rukh had more knotty problems with this project. Aditya wanted Shah Rukh because until then he hadn't played a romantic hero. His most successful films had featured him as an anti-hero. Kajol and Shah Rukh had been established as a successful screen pair with *Baazigar* (*Gambler*, 1993), but the film was a thriller. During the making of *Darr*, Aditya had talked to Shah Rukh about making a film called *Auzaar* (*Weapon*). Shah Rukh assumed that a film with this name would be a 'macho, cool dude' kind of movie. Instead Aditya had narrated a love story.

Shah Rukh thought that romances were 'pansy', effete. He wasn't interested in singing songs in pretty locations and then eloping with the girl, as was the Bollywood norm. Besides, the other two Khan heroes – Aamir and Salman – were playing the lover boy roles with great success, and Shah Rukh was happy to be regarded as a hatke (different) actor. Over three weeks and several meetings, Aditya tried to convince the reluctant star.

In their fourth meeting, Aditya told Shah Rukh that he was indeed a star, but he would never achieve superstar status unless he was every woman's dream man and every mother's dream son. *DDLJ* could make him that. As Shah Rukh dithered, Aditya thought of alternatives – perhaps Saif Ali Khan, the son of leading actress Sharmila Tagore, would fit the bill. But one day, at Mehboob studios, outside the sets of *Karan Arjun* (1995), Shah Rukh finally agreed to do Aditya's film.

For Simran's mother, Lajjo, Aditya selected a fine but underrated character actress, Farida Jalal. Farida had returned to films via television, after an eight-year post-marriage gap. Her old-world charm and serenity were the perfect foil to Simran's stern father, Baldev. For Baldev, Aditya had zeroed in on Amrish Puri, who until then was mostly famous for playing villainous roles. Amrish, with his piercing eyes and large build, had a towering personality. Yash would have preferred to cast their close friend Anupam Kher in this role, but Aditya wouldn't budge. Eventually Yash offered the role to Amrish, and Anupam was given the important but less pivotal role of Raj's father.

Casting Kuljeet, Simran's chauvinist Punjabi

fiancé, was also tricky. Aditya had talked to Armaan Kohli, the son of producer Raj Kumar Kohli. Armaan was trying to become a hero, but repeated flops had stymied his ambitions. So he agreed to be the baddie – the Yash Raj banner was worth the image change. Meanwhile, a television actor named Parmeet Sethi was lobbying fiercely for the role. Parmeet was a tall, strapping Punjabi who until then had played good guys in television serials. He now couldn't persuade Aditya that he could become a convincing bad guy. Eventually Armaan backed out, and Aditya called Parmeet for a screen test.

Screen tests are not a routine casting process in Bollywood. At any given time, at least a dozen producers are chasing the handful of saleable stars, rendering screen tests unnecessary. Only the minor character actors have to give screen tests. Parmeet prepared for the test as if his career depended on it. First Parmeet and his wife Archana Puran Singh, also an actress and television star, injected Punjabi flavour into the dialogue. A small-town Punjabi would hardly speak in straightforward urban Hindi. So Punjabi colloquialisms like chak-de-phatte ('go for the kill') were added. Parmeet also dressed for the part, wearing boots, jeans and a waistcoat.

Aditya was impressed by both his passion and his performance. Parmeet became Kuljeet.

The film's title came from Kiron Kher, Anupam's wife. The line is part of a popular Hindi film song from the film *Chor Machaye Shor* (*The Boisterous Thief,* 1974).[37] Three years before *DDLJ* was conceived, Kiron had mentioned the title to Aditya – she was going to use it for a script she had written. The line stuck in Aditya's mind – he thought it had passion, masti (mischievousness) and a flair perfect for his young romance. He asked Kiron if he could use it instead. She agreed and added jokingly that Aditya should credit her. *DDLJ* is perhaps the only film ever with a 'Title suggested by' credit.

THE SOUNDTRACK

As he cast the film, Aditya also created the songs. He was clear that his music had to be bubble-gum, youthful pop in the Western mode, but also purely Indian – a mix of the old masters R.D. Burman and Shankar–Jaikishan. He selected the brothers Jatin and Lalit Pundit to create this music. Jatin–Lalit, as these composers are called, come from an illustrious music gharana (house). Their uncle

Pundit Jasraj is a celebrated classical singer, and their sister Sulakshna, an actress, has also sung playback for films. Like the rest of the team, Jatin–Lalit were young – thirty-four and twenty-eight respectively – and hungry. They had composed the soundtrack for several movies, but hadn't yet found the one blockbuster that would propel them into the stratosphere.

Jatin–Lalit had earlier done a music sitting with Yash, in which they had played several tunes. Yash had an untrained but keen ear for music, and the brothers were anxiously trying to please him. They barely noticed Aditya sitting in the corner. The session ended with Yash promising that he would work with the boys, but for a year nothing happened. Then one day, they were recording a song at the Sunny sound studio, when they got a call from Aditya. He asked them to come immediately to his office. Aditya offered them *DDLJ*, but he wanted to do one sitting first to make sure that they were professionally in synch. He also wanted to use one of the tunes they had played for his father, *'Payal bacha ke chalna'* (Save your anklets as you walk), which eventually became the chartbuster *'Mehndi lagake rakhna'* (Put your henna on).

Aditya's script bowled the brothers over. The heated romance and the backdrop of the wedding created perfect situations for songs. They were convinced that this was the film that would push them into the big league. Jatin–Lalit started creating the music. Aditya sat with them in the initial sessions, tinkering and twisting until he was happy. When a tune was ready, the three would take it to Yash and Pamela. For every tune selected, five were rejected.

For Bollywood soundtracks, tunes are usually created first and then words are written to the music. Yash was a renowned connoisseur of poetry. He had had a long-standing friendship with the legendary lyricist Sahir Ludhianvi. Ludhianvi, an eccentric genius, wrote the lyrics for all of Yash's films, from the first in 1959 until his death in 1980.[38] After Sahir, Yash worked with several renowned lyricists, including Javed Akhtar and the late Anand Bakshi. Anand had joined the Yash Raj crew with *Chandni*, in 1989. Anand was a more prosaic poet than Sahir Ludhianvi. But he had an incredible dexterity and range.

Aditya's first sitting with Anand, then a sixty-six-year-old veteran with writing credits in 534 films, was disastrous. Anand loved the script and, after a narration, he told Aditya that if his film could capture even 50 per cent of the story, it would be a great film. But Anand, who had authored approximately 2,700 songs till then,[39] couldn't write one verse that satisfied the debutant director. The song situation had Simran cavorting in her house, singing about her unseen lover. Aditya was insistent that the words be 'young-sounding', something that a girl in London would sing. After four days of struggle and twenty-four rejected verses, Anand suggested that Aditya find himself another lyricist. But Aditya persisted. And finally Anand came up with *'Mere khwabon mein jo aaye'* (He who comes in my dreams). It was the first song of the film, and on 15 August 1994, became the first song recorded for the film.

For dialogue too, Aditya insisted on 'young-sounding', everyday language. He wanted unforced, natural speech, not the usual melodramatic, grandstanding dialogue-baazi or dialogue-slinging. Javed Siddiqui, an acclaimed playwright who had written over fifty films, including Yash's *Darr*, was hired. But Aditya wasn't satisfied. Javed's language was too ornate. Aditya believed that Javed's sensibility was inherently too refined to create the unlearned freshness that he was looking for. So two weeks before shooting started, Aditya rewrote some of his scenes, selecting lines from Javed and adding his own. As the shooting loomed nearer, Aditya and his assistants started doing trial runs. With Karan posing as Farida and Uday as Kajol, Aditya rehearsed his camera movements. They blocked shots in Aditya's bedroom, in preparation for the shoot, which was to begin on 6 September.

THE SHOOT

Making movies in India is sweaty, dirty, hard work. Mumbai's studios are functional but not luxurious. The shooting floors are dusty, the bathrooms are barely usable, and the noise levels are uncomfortably high. The hot lights and army of toiling technicians soon turn a set into a furnace. It's controlled chaos.

Films are hardly ever shot in start-to-finish schedules. Actors work on more than one film at a time, and cannot be available for three months at a stretch.[40] Also, an actor's work doesn't end when the shooting is finished. Most Mumbai movies aren't made in synch sound, because there is too much ambient sound. After principal photography is over, actors have to dub their dialogue.[41] Shooting schedules are usually coordinated around the availability of the hero and heroine. *DDLJ* was shot in five-, ten- and twenty-day schedules from September 1994 to August 1995.

Despite the heat and dust, Bollywood shootings often have a carnival-like atmosphere, with relatives, guests, and other producers and directors dropping in to visit. But Aditya, who according to Karan was 'a tyrant on the sets', wanted no distractions. His sets were closed. Even the family tiptoed in. When the shooting was in Mumbai, Yash would drop in to have lunch with the unit. Sometimes Pamela brought home-cooked food. Sometimes she also spruced up the sets – fixing the props in Simran's kitchen set or placing a teddy bear in her bedroom.

The *DDLJ* set had a cosy, home-like atmosphere. The team, apart from Yash and Manmohan, was shockingly young. At twenty-three, Aditya was the boss. Instead of a rigid, top-heavy power structure, there was a more informal working relationship. Egos and tantrums were held in check. Despite the pressure-cooker atmosphere of shooting, a certain joie de vivre prevailed.

Shah Rukh and Kajol have a thriving professional relationship. Their on-screen chemistry comes, in part, from their off-screen comfort with each other.[42] At times the camaraderie became disruptive. While shooting a critical love scene in Switzerland, both actors got the giggles. Neither Shah Rukh nor Kajol could keep a straight face through it. Every time Shah Rukh pulled down his jacket zipper to show Kajol lipstick marks, both of them burst out laughing. After running through three magazines of raw stock, Aditya lost his patience. He took a five-minute break and firmly told them to get it together. Then he did one more take. Shah Rukh and Kajol managed to hold off their giggles long enough to do the scene, and then started laughing again.

Aditya was strict with his crew but he pampered his actors. He decided that at the beginning of each schedule, his actors would be greeted with flowers and a welcome note in their make-up room. He wanted them to know that this wasn't just another film. Single-stem roses and crystal vases were bought and placed for each actor. But after the first schedule, the struggle of making movies made niceties impossible.

Aditya's clarity gave the actors confidence. Every day, he carried a blue file, which contained his handwritten notes on structure and shot breakdowns, but he rarely opened it. He knew exactly how he wanted to shoot. For a debutant director, his precision was startling. Aditya rarely acted out scenes for his artistes. He had given all the leading players detailed narrations, and before each shot he would brief them. He would read the scene, explaining the points of emphasis and the body language he was looking for. The actor then took it further.

Amrish's first day on the shoot required him to do a prayer scene. The sequence, which was eventually edited out, established that Baldev conducts morning prayers, which the family attends, and for which Simran is always late. Just as they were ready to take the shot, Amrish asked Aditya what time it was. Aditya, perplexed, told him. But Amrish wanted to know the exact time in the film that Baldev was conducting the prayer. Aditya hadn't given this any thought and it took him a few minutes to figure it out. He couldn't understand the relevance of the question. He thought the senior actor was just testing him.

Later in the day, they canned a sequence in which Baldev returns home fuming about decadent NRI (non-resident Indian) children being a blot on Indian culture. Aditya wanted Amrish to climb halfway up the stairs and then begin to speak. Amrish wanted to know why it was necessary to be on the stairs. Aditya, despite his age and inexperience, wasn't intimidated. He persisted and eventually, after several minutes of discussion, Amrish did the scene as Aditya had visualized it. Later on, Amrish told Yash that Aditya was a good director because he knew exactly what he wanted. Amrish didn't question Aditya again. He says, 'Within a couple of days, I formed my opinion that Aditya was far superior to so many directors, both new and established.'

Aditya's aim was to follow the screenplay as closely as he could. The writer in him led the director. Like Yash, he wasn't interested in flashy technique but in telling the story well. Before every shot, Aditya would consult his cinematographer, Manmohan. Manmohan, a quietly efficient technician, has been co-architect of Yash's soft-focus romances since *Faasle*. But unlike Yash, Aditya wasn't as committed to beauty and glamour. He wanted a more natural mise en scène. Since Aditya had assisted in many of the films that Manmohan had shot, they worked together smoothly. Aditya would discuss options on each shot with Manmohan, and then make a decision. At times, Aditya was tempted to try some snazzy camerawork. But he opted for simplicity instead.

Aditya isn't quite the creator of female beauty that his father is. The Yash Chopra woman, an ethereal goddess dressed in pastel chiffons, is part of Bollywood's vocabulary. Aditya's idea of an attractive woman is more prosaic. He prefers a jhalli (unkempt) woman. So he entrusted glamour to Karan and his friend Manish Malhotra. Karan, an aesthete from his toddler days, became the 'costume-in-charge'. He spent hours agonizing over bangles and dupattas. Sometimes, he would rush to suburban Mumbai to buy bindis that would match the day's outfits. Pamela also chipped in. For the several older women characters – mother, grandmother, aunts – she bought brocades and Phulkari dupattas from Delhi.

Manish designed the costumes. Manish, a self-taught designer, loved fashion and films equally. He had started designing film costumes in 1990. A few months before *DDLJ* was released, Manish became a star with *Rangeela* (*Colourful*, 1995), a heavily stylized, flashy love triangle in which

Manish revamped the image of heroine Urmila Matondkar from erstwhile child star into sex goddess. But when Aditya offered him *DDLJ*, Manish was still an upcoming designer working out of a small workshop at the Geetanjali dubbing studio. At first Manish was in charge of the Western clothes – Aditya had only narrated the first half to him. But as the film progressed, the Chopras were impressed by Manish's innate flair for design and Aditya narrated the second half as well.

Manish was bubbling with new ideas. Even in the traditional Indian clothes he wanted to try new colours and styles. Aditya was equally adamant about keeping it 'simple'. He didn't want the audience to be distracted by the clothes. He didn't want it to be a 'Yash Chopra fantasy'. At times, Aditya went with Manish's ideas, but sometimes he was – as he puts it – 'stupidly stuck'. So Manish would try and convince Aditya via Pamela. Yash also supervised the Indian clothes. He was finicky and obsessed with detail. And Yash could only decide on a costume once the artist was wearing it. Sketches or clothes on a hanger meant little.

For *'Mehndi lagake rakhna'*, a boisterous song-and-dance number celebrating Simran and

Kuljeet's engagement, Manish suggested green for Simran's outfit. Traditionally, Punjabi brides wear reds or maroons. The bolder ones might opt for pink, but green was unheard of. Aditya was upset and had several heated discussions with Manish. But Manish was convinced that a shaded green lachha kurta would be distinctive and attractive. Finally Aditya conceded.

Sometimes, the convictions went awry. In the club number '*Rukh ja*' (Stop), Manish opted for a tight gown, which made Kajol look more podgy than elegant.[43] Of course Kajol – who has absolutely no interest in fashion or preening – didn't make things easier. She refused to lose weight or let the hairdresser straighten her hair. She also hated wearing wigs and jewellery. In some scenes, the fine hair on her upper lip showed. Karan was constantly devising ways to make her look slimmer. While shooting on the roads in Switzerland, he would himself comb her hair between takes.

Besides functioning as costume czar and all-purpose bouncing board, Karan also acted. He played Raj's friend Ponchy, and was mostly relegated to having his cap knocked off by Shah Rukh. But he had one key scene in which he goes to Baldev's store to buy beer. Baldev refuses, and when Ponchy persists he starts to get angry. Karan had rehearsed the scene, but after the shot was done, he asked for another take. Amrish looked surprised while Aditya just laughed. But both let Karan have one more go. Ironically, Uday – who secretly wanted to act – didn't get the chance. Uday took care of the clap and continuity, and was also prop master.

But perhaps Aditya's best assistant was Yash. Yash provided moral and monetary support, but he relinquished power to his son. Aditya, not he, was the captain. Yash's brand equity and connections made things fall into place. Whatever Aditya wanted – a church in Switzerland, a helicopter, Swiss police for one scene – he got. Throughout the shoot, Yash hovered in the background – a guardian angel who could smooth out rough spots. Sometimes Yash also made creative suggestions. Aditya listened to him like he listened to other technical crew, and then did exactly what he wanted.

But even Yash's mythical powers couldn't conjure up the field of yellow flowers that Aditya wanted. Aditya had always known that the colour of his film was yellow. He had visualized Raj and Simran reuniting in a swaying field of sarson, yellow mustard flowers. The image of Raj, in his Harley-Davidson jacket standing in the quintessentially Punjabi sarson, encapsulated *DDLJ*'s Western-look-Eastern-values message. The trouble was that there was no mustard to be found.

Three weeks before his January schedule, Aditya was scouting for sarson. Yash, Manmohan and Aditya travelled through Punjab, but sarson proved elusive. There were occasional patches of flowers, but not the sea of yellow that Aditya was looking for. Finally a local suggested looking in neighbouring Gurgaon. Aditya, by now disheartened and exhausted, wasn't interested, but Yash suggested that since it was on their way, they should stop by. Gurgaon was exactly what Aditya wanted – carpets of yellow flowers with a train track going through it. He couldn't stop smiling. Aditya had everything he wanted. Almost.

Aditya's clarity and hard work didn't impress Saroj Khan. Saroj, who had been working in Bollywood since she was three years old, was a consummate choreographer. Her career spanned generations of heroines. Saroj had worked as a group dancer with Madhubala and Vyjayanthimala in the 1950s, and had established herself as a choreographer in the 1980s, working with heroines like Sridevi and Madhuri Dixit. With songs becoming a critical element in the marketing of films, and even determining the success of some films, choreographers were increasingly becoming powerful players in the film industry. In the early 1990s, Saroj had little competition. Bollywood, literally, danced to her tune.

Saroj and Aditya didn't – or couldn't – connect. Aditya thought she was brilliant at the traditional Indian numbers, but unlike many directors he wasn't willing to give her a free rein. He wanted his songs to be part of the screenplay and not isolated 'items', Bollywood lingo for lavish dance numbers that serve as attractive diversions from the story. Aditya would come to the set with his shot divisions ready for the songs. He also insisted on being the one to call 'cut' on all takes, even when a song was being shot under the supervision of a choreographer. 'She probably thought I was overbearing,' he says. Saroj knew Aditya from his days as an assistant on *Chandni*. 'I didn't think he was so capable of directing a movie,' she says. Karan puts it more bluntly: 'She thought we were doing rubbish. It was "Yash Chopra's son gone mad."'

Their differences came to a head while shooting *'Mehndi lagake rakhna'* in February 1995. Aditya was insistent that Simran, the bride-to-be, would only dance towards the end of the number. Saroj thought Aditya was taking the life out of a robust song. After all, she argued, Yash himself had started the tradition of brides dancing at their engagements with Sridevi in *Chandni*. To make matters worse, Karan independently decided to make alterations in the costumes of the group dancers. He thought a hearty, Punjabi dance with men waving scarves in each hand was a cliché. Two scarves were predictable, but one was stylish. Saroj was livid that her dancers' costumes had been changed without her permission. The scarves were restored (after Karan was berated by both Saroj and Aditya), but the song was shot as Aditya had visualized it: Simran sits coyly while Raj dances.

The rocky relationship reached a breaking point in Switzerland. Saroj, shooting in France for another film, came late for the *DDLJ* shoot. She recalls it being 'two hours'. Aditya says it was three days. He refused to stop work for anyone. He tried to get another choreographer – Shah Rukh called Farah Khan in London at 6 a.m. one morning – but she was committed to another film. So Aditya decided to film the song himself. He had just started doing a small sequence featuring Shah Rukh and Kajol on a bridge when Saroj showed up. She apologized but Aditya decided that he would never work with her again.

Farah joined the *DDLJ* unit for the last song, '*Rukh ja*'. Saroj, older and less sophisticated, had never become one of the *DDLJ* gang; she attributes it to a generation gap. But Farah, young and trendy, fitted in effortlessly. She was as Karan put it, 'so not Saroj'. Farah was perfect for '*Rukh ja*', a foot-tapping number Raj sings in a Paris nightclub. Above everything, the song had to be cool. Farah, Manish and Sharmishtha put their heads together. Instead of using the regular union dancers, Farah hired young, slim college girls, who wore minidresses and thigh-high garter socks imported from London. The set would include a giant backlit vinyl screen with the Parisian skyline printed on it. Aditya wanted MTV-style slickness.

Except that Shah Rukh didn't have the time. Date problems led to Shah Rukh doing double shifts – that is, he was shooting for two films at a time. From 11 a.m. to 3 p.m., he was shooting

DDLJ, and from 3 p.m. to 10 p.m., he was working for Subhash Ghai's *Trimurti* (*Trinity,* 1995). Aditya was furious at the situation, but he had little choice. He had four days to finish the song. So Farah improvised. Instead of MTV, she went back to the dancing king of an earlier generation – Shammi Kapoor. She updated Shammi's strange beatnik-meets-groovy-twister-meets-Indian-lothario dancing style from the classic *Teesri Manzil* (*Third Floor,* 1966). Instead of flashy nanosecond cuts, Farah did long shots. She also threw in an opera singer and Karan. *'Rukh ja'* wasn't what Aditya had visualized, but it had an infectious energy that worked.[44] The song created a collaborative team that refashioned Bollywood songs in the 1990s.

Through the editing, Aditya didn't show a single frame of *DDLJ* to Yash. Unlike other Indian directors, who solicit innumerable pre-release critiques, Aditya works with blinkers on. In early August, the family and Manmohan saw rushes at Rajkamal studio. The film was unfinished – the climax still had to be shot. The reaction was positive but not overwhelmingly so. The screening was followed by a dinner at the posh China Garden restaurant, but the mood was sombre. There was great apprehension about the climax. Bollywood audiences expect their heroes to be supermen who carry the girl off into the sunset, not guys who give speeches, shed tears and then are willing to leave the girl with her father. Would such an anti-climactic climax work?

As before, Aditya followed his instincts. This was the scene he had written the film for – he wasn't going to change it. Aditya rehearsed the scene and shot it in one day. The final action sequence at the railway station was shot in Panvel. With shooting complete, Aditya rushed into post-production. They had decided to release the film in October, around the Diwali festival, and there was hardly any time.[45] Dubbing had already begun. Yash was perturbed at the film's length – three hours and fourteen minutes. He helped Aditya shave off two-and-a-half minutes.[46] On 21 August Jatin–Lalit started work on the background music. They were given only ten days. For mixing, Aditya shifted base to the Prasad laboratories in Chennai. On 30 September, the film's first copy was printed.

The Box Office

The next day, the Chopras, Karan, Karan's mother Hiroo and a few of Aditya's friends flew to Chennai to see the film. This time, there was no second opinion. Everybody loved *DDLJ*. 'I was just ecstatic,' recalls Pamela. 'For the first time in my life I could not talk for three quarters of an hour after seeing the film. It was so brilliant.' The rest of the crew saw the film on 8 October. The universal reaction was unstinting praise.

But Aditya's work wasn't over. He was busy cutting trailers. Inspired by Hollywood films, Aditya also decided to make a thirty-minute television show on the making of *DDLJ*. It was the perfect way to market a film, and it hadn't been done before.[47] Uday and Karan were entrusted with the project. They had been recording, on video, the goings-on while the film was being made, and had eight hours of tapes. They now edited these tapes down, and on 18 October, *The Making of DDLJ* was aired on Doordarshan, the national channel. It created a splash. In places like Assam, shops closed because people thought that they were showing the actual film.

As D-Day neared, Aditya's calm occasionally cracked. During the preview show for the unit at Rajkamal studio, he was hit by pre-release panic. What if he had made a bad film? He left the show and walked around the studio for twenty minutes, coming back only after the interval was over. He didn't want to hear any comments that the audience might have made. Meanwhile, *DDLJ*'s soundtrack was notching up excellent sales. A film's soundtrack is usually released three months before the film, and helps to bring in the 'initial' or first-weekend audience. *DDLJ* sold between one and 1.5 million tapes pre-release. The signs were positive, but in the movie business success is uncertain and failure looms large. Days before release, a senior employee in Yash Raj hesitatingly asked Javed Siddiqui, 'You are an experienced man. Do you think this travelogue will run?'

The travelogue ran from the first show. The advance booking, which opened on the Monday before release, was tremendous. Anil Thadani, who was distributing the film in the Bombay territory, recalls going to the Gaiety-Galaxy theatres in suburban Mumbai. At 9.30 a.m., over 700 people thronged the theatre to buy tickets. Anil called Pamela, who came to see the crowds. She was in tears. *DDLJ*'s first weekend was sold out.

Aditya was sleeping when his film's first show started at twelve noon on 20 October 1995. For years, he had seen other directors' movies in the first show, but he decided to skip his own. He wasn't interested in seeing the first half because he knew there was enough masala to keep the audience entertained. Aditya was worried about the climax. In the twentieth reel, Shah Rukh would give a long speech with tears in his eyes. If the audience hooted or even got restless, *DDLJ* was sunk. Aditya and his third assistant Sameer entered the Gaiety theatre just after the interval. When Shah Rukh's speech began, Aditya crossed his fingers and put his head between his knees. There was complete silence. The audience was hanging on to every word Shah Rukh said. Aditya was home, safe.

In a few weeks, they were mouthing the words along with Shah Rukh. The repeat audience had already started. Shah Rukh, shooting in Jaipur for a film called *Chahat* (*Love*, 1996), went into a local theatre with his director Mahesh Bhatt and heroine Pooja Bhatt. Mahesh hadn't seen the film, and he was curious about the latest blockbuster. In the climax, mumbling started and Shah Rukh panicked. Perhaps he wasn't holding them as an actor. But as it got louder he could hear the audience clearly – they were just saying his lines with him.

For once, even the critics were pleased. In the *Times of India,* Khalid Mohamed wrote, 'Popular, high-cost cinema has come of age.' *Screen,* a weekly, declared, 'A young master arrives.' The trade magazines, of course, were ecstatically recording the booming box office. *Film Information* noted that *DDLJ* had created '... new records at most places ... It is being patronized by ladies and youngsters in a big way and is set for a long and meritorious run everywhere.' In Mumbai, every show in every theatre in the first week was full except for one Saturday evening show, which had 100-odd seats empty. Distributors across the country called elatedly about the collections. Aditya took it all in, pleased but not euphoric.

His sights were set higher. Aditya wasn't just aiming to make a hit film. He was aiming to make a film that was as big as *Hum Aapke Hain Koun...?* Anil recalls that Aditya always maintained that if his film 'did even one rupee less than *Hum Aapke Hain Koun...?',* he would be disappointed. For five to six weeks, Aditya tracked collections. When the numbers stood steady, he allowed himself to breathe more easily. Before he started *DDLJ,* Aditya had told his family that he wouldn't take a holiday until he had made a successful film. In December, when *DDLJ* was a confirmed blockbuster, the Chopras went to Bali. In the long run, *DDLJ* didn't equal *Hum Aapke Hain Koun*'s collections but it did make the list of the ten most successful Hindi movies ever.

DDLJ was Yash Raj Films' biggest success. Aditya was transformed from a nondescript assistant to hotshot director. What had taken Yash decades, Aditya had achieved with one film. But at the Chopra house, the elation was tinged with bitterness. In the weeks after the film's release, a controversy erupted that made the painfully media-shy Aditya into gossip magazine fodder. It soured *DDLJ*'s success then, and continues to rankle years later.

Honey Irani and Pamela had been friends for twenty-two years. Honey had been married to writer Javed Akhtar, who had scripted many of Yash's films. Their children had grown up together. Uday and Farhan were close friends. After her divorce, Honey's fledgling writing career had found wing in Yash Raj Films. Her first script was *Lamhe*. She had also written *Aaina* (*Mirror*) and *Darr* and had had meetings with Aditya during which they had worked on the *DDLJ* screenplay. But Honey's name does not appear on the *DDLJ* credits.

Beyond this, the facts are foggy. The month before the film released, a tug of war over writing credits ensued. Aditya maintains that Honey's contribution to *DDLJ* was minuscule – he says that he only had four sessions with her, and then wrote the film on his own. So Yash decided to give Aditya a solo credit for the story and screenplay. Honey disagrees vehemently. She says they had several 7 a.m. meetings on *DDLJ* and she even accompanied the unit for the Switzerland schedule. While she concedes that Aditya had done 'quite a lot of work' on the story, she says she helped to flesh out the narrative and add details. 'Even if 80 per cent of the screenplay was his, at least 20 per cent was mine,' Honey says. 'Don't take that 20 per cent away from me.'

Pamela, who was abroad when the trouble started, tried to make peace. But the media added fuel to the fire. Gossip magazines carried shrill headlines about stolen credit. Aditya remained silent, but Pamela and Honey exchanged accusations and counter-accusations in print. A misunderstanding between friends snowballed into a hurtful controversy. Their professional and personal relationship was irretrievably damaged. Honey never worked with the company again. Aditya didn't heal either. He says: 'All my life I hoped and craved for my share of the spotlight, for a day when hopefully people will think of me as a talented person. And that day came but I never enjoyed it because I always wondered how many people have this doubt in their minds that this is not my work.'

DDLJ's dialogue writer, Javed Siddiqui, also parted ways with the Chopras. Again, the bone of contention was credit. Aditya, who says he rewrote much of the film's dialogue, took the credit of 'additional dialogue'. Siddiqui insists that his writing was hardly changed – Aditya only wrote some lines, which were added while shooting in Switzerland. Siddiqui felt that the joint credit was 'an injustice'. And though he maintains that Yash and Aditya are 'fantastic makers', he left the company.

In February 1996, at the forty-first annual *Filmfare* awards, when *DDLJ* won for best dialogue, Siddiqui and Aditya walked on stage together. The *Filmfare* awards, instituted by the *Filmfare* magazine, are Bollywood's oldest awards.

They don't carry the prestige or box office clout of the Oscars, but they are Bollywood's biggest bash. That evening, *DDLJ* swept the awards, taking home a total of eleven statuettes.[48] Among others, Aditya won best director, Yash (as producer) won for best film, Shah Rukh and Kajol won for best performances.

After the *Filmfare* awards party, an inebriated Saroj rang the bell at the Chopra bungalow. It was past midnight. Saroj had been nominated for the choreography of *'Mehndi'* but she hadn't won. She had come to apologize. She said sorry to Aditya for underestimating him. But she never saw *DDLJ*, and neither did she work with him again. A few months later, *DDLJ* won the National Award, a prestigious prize instituted by the government and given by the president. Aditya sent Yash to collect it.

Despite the laurels, Aditya remained reclusive. He made Yash his representative at award functions and Bollywood parties. Apart from one interview to *Filmfare* magazine about winning their award, he did not speak to the media. He also refused to be photographed, so magazines were forced to use stray, decades-old pictures of him. Aditya was hailed as the voice of a new generation and hounded for

On 20 October 1995, Yash Raj Films released
Dilwale Dulhania Le Jayenge (DDLJ), and
with it created a modern classic.

Raj Malhotra, a brash, twenty-something, meets Simran Singh, a traditional Indian girl brought up in Southall. They meet on a Eurail trip, fight first, fall in love later.

Simran, though, is already engaged and is whisked off to India by her father, Chaudhry Baldev Singh. Raj follows Simran, wins over the family, refuses to elope, and insists on seeking permission from her father.

With *DDLJ*, the NRI or non-resident Indian took centre stage. The film's protagonists were second-generation NRIs who demolished the Bollywood cliché that Western ideas corrupt minds.

The movie also launched Shah Rukh Khan and Kajol's careers in a way that none of their previous films had. It also established them as the younger generation's lead romantic pair. Over the years, this pairing is included in the list of greats like Rekha–Amitabh Bachchan, Nargis–Raj Kapoor, Sharmila Tagore–Rajesh Khanna.

DDLJ was shot in five-, ten- and twenty-day schedules from September 1994 to August 1995. The set had a cosy, home-like atmosphere but was distraction free. The team, apart from Yash Chopra and the cinematographer Manmohan Singh, was shockingly young. At twenty-three, Aditya was the boss.

interviews, but he made no exceptions. Aditya Chopra became a name, but not a face.

The distinction was critical. Aditya explains, 'The purity of *DDLJ* came because I see films for just the love of films. I love films and the charm of going to the theatre, buying a ticket, buying popcorn and waiting for the film to start. That is my greatest high. Nothing gives me more pleasure than that. It is largely responsible for the kind of film I made. It gives me a lot of respect for the audience. I never want to fake an emotion or cheat them. I can only be sincere when I am one of the audience. I firmly believe that if I cannot sit in the theatre as a common person, I'll be finished.'

So, one of the most successful directors in India has remained almost invisible.[49]

Four

Believable Fantasies

The millions who grew up in post-Independence India lived very far from the rest of the world. A centralized socialist economy and an enormous Soviet-style planning structure filled the markets with products a good two or three decades behind the West. That is, when you could find what you were looking for – strict quotas created artificial shortages, and also overstocking of products that nobody wanted. Businessmen and entrepreneurs had to navigate through forests of regulations and permits and government departments, all of which made up the 'licence raj'. Trying to set up the simplest business deal could require permissions from half a dozen ministries. Of course, bribery and the use of 'contacts' were standard operating procedures in this environment. Films were censored, especially foreign ones. Television was strictly state-controlled, and prime-time programming often featured farmers and crusty-looking agricultural scientists talking about seeds. Indians dreamed of foreign countries, and especially America, as one dreams of a faraway heaven.

In 1991, under the threat of imminent economic collapse, and facing an inability to repay World Bank loans, the government introduced wide-ranging economic reforms that dismantled the licence raj, deregulated various industries and allowed multinationals entry into the country. India, a traditional and sleepy society mired in thousands of years of history, was thrust headlong into globalization. In the same year satellite television – BBC World Service, MTV, Star Plus – arrived. In the years that followed, India underwent an enormous cultural churning that, like the fabled amrit manthan (churning for nectar) of the gods, spewed out both nectar and poison.

Suddenly the landscape was awash with foreign labels. Coca-Cola, McDonald's, Levi's – what was once the prerogative of only those who could afford to travel abroad was now available at the local store. Suddenly a plethora of channels offered dizzying alternatives to the staid, monotonous government-run television programming. Urban Indians (some 225 million people)[50] watched soap operas like *The Bold and the Beautiful* in their bedrooms. The West, with its promise of a glittering, flashy, modern lifestyle, entered the inner sanctums of middle-class Indian homes.

Liberalization brought the middle class, with their increased spending power, to the fore. But the rapid changes also brought confusion. Scriptwriter Javed Akhtar says, 'We didn't know how much of the old to keep and how much to replace. What should we do – leave Coke and drink only lassi? Throw out our jeans and wear lungis? This modern world was dazzling, but if we gave in, would it sweep our foundations away?'

In a consumerist culture, the old rules no longer held. In *The Great Indian Middle Class*, author Pavan K. Varma writes:

> The institution which is under ceaseless pressure is the home. The demise of the joint family has given place to the nuclear family where

> traditional family values of support and a sense
> of belonging and togetherness have often given
> way to individual pursuits and ambitions.[51]

Varma conclude that the relentless consumerism and increased competition had led the middle class to 'a growing neurosis, both at a personal and collective level'.[52] Indeed, stress, depression, divorce, long considered to be ailments of the affluent West, started to become common in India.[53] In December 1992, the demolition of the Babri Masjid by Hindu fundamentalists and the subsequent bomb blasts and riots in Mumbai also pointed out the deep schisms and reactionary trends in the country. Underneath the shiny new image of a progressive nation being absorbed willingly into the currents of globalization, there was a complex matrix of poverty, corruption, chauvinism and violence. Scriptwriter Anjum Rajabali says, 'Basic questions came up. What is India? Who is Indian?'

DDLJ offered a definition, a purposefully naive, sugar-coated one, but a definition all the same. *DDLJ* told Indians that an Indian is a hybrid who easily enjoys the material comforts of the West and the spiritual comforts of the East. In the push and pull of a liberalized economy, this synthesis was a comfortable answer. You didn't have to choose between the two – the twain could meet, without friction or confusion. So Raj, in his Harley-Davidson leather jacket, is a conformist, and Simran, despite the occasional miniskirt, is a virgin. Like fusion clothes and fusion food, *DDLJ* presented a fusion lifestyle. Karan Johar took it further in *Kuch Kuch Hota Hai* (*Something Happens*, 1998), creating a fairy-tale Neverland in which prayers and Polosport clothing blend seamlessly without conflict. *DDLJ*'s world is also airbrushed, but the realistic dialogue and textured characterizations moored the film in recognizable, everyday life. *DDLJ* created what director Govind Nihalani calls 'believable fantasies'.[54]

The insecurities thrown up by a fast-changing culture were assuaged by a retreat into traditional values. So *DDLJ*, like *Hum Aapke Hain Koun...?*, conceived of the family as sacrosanct. In these narratives, the family – extended, not nuclear – is the centre, the basis, of all that is properly Indian. Personal desire and parental authority must be reconciled. Raj and Simran achieve their goal by finally restoring the status quo. If you try hard enough, *DDLJ* said, you can have both, the person you love and family approval, and enjoy the 'arranged love marriage'.[55]

The message found a receptive audience in Indian urban youth, for whom rebellion seems to have become increasingly passé. A 1997 MTV survey, 'Tuning into Indian Youth', which polled 450 respondents in three cities, confirmed that the outwardly modern, inwardly traditional mode prescribed by the film was prevalent in the culture at large. Sixty-four per cent of the respondents said that it was 'important to uphold traditional values'. In 1999, the survey was conducted again with 2,745 respondents in six cities. This time, 65.63 per cent of the respondents agreed with the statement, 'I try to obey my elders even if it hurts,' and only 29.33 per cent of them said yes when asked: 'Is premarital sex a way of life in the 1990s?' Raj, smart enough to play by society's rules and also fulfil his individual desires, became a youth icon. In the 1999 survey, Shah Rukh was voted a leading role model.

DDLJ worked as a fantasy for Indian audiences both inside and outside India. For the local audience, the film offered a lifestyle to aspire to. Aditya continued in Yash's time-honoured tradition of 'glamorous realism'.[56] *DDLJ* is less flamboyant than the typical Yash film like *Lamhe,* but it offers the same seductive mix of foreign locations, flashy cars and mansions. After all, Raj is a millionaire's son. Significantly, at the end of the film, Simran and Raj return to London where they will presumably enjoy a lavish life with all the perks of the modern West, while Baldev and family stay back in the more spartan Punjab. But the film also reassured the home audience that while their expatriate brethren might enjoy the affluence of the West, their hearts ached for the lost homeland. Finally, India is the reservoir of moral values. As Kuljeet's father says, 'Go east, go west, Punjab is the best.'

For the expatriate audience, *DDLJ* painted a rose-tinted fantasy of India. In the film, Punjab wasn't a killing field stained with blood by both terrorists and security forces, but a rural Utopia. Here colourfully dressed Sikhs played musical instruments in swaying fields, and homes were filled with large, loving families. The film fed the NRI nostalgia for traditions and rituals like Karva Chauth. It also reassured them that the West had not and could not change India irrevocably. It could not rob them of their roots. These NRIs often clung to the India that they had left behind decades ago, that they nurtured in their imaginations. They were more traditionally Indian than the Indians living at home. *DDLJ* told them that you could, as an *India Today* article stated, 'straddle both worlds, have your cake – and your green card – and eat it too'.[57]

Even in terms of its own form, *DDLJ* artfully combined the traditional and the new. Somewhere in Switzerland, in between takes, Kajol, giggling, said to Aditya: 'I thought your film was different.' Aditya replied, only half-joking, 'My film is not different. I'm making the most commercial, clichéd, tapori (pedestrian) movie. I'm making the oldest story in the world.'

The Hindi film romance follows a formula. Boy meets girl, boy loses girl, boy wins girl. These films rarely explore the inevitably messy complications of relationships, marriage or sexuality. Lust, betrayal, insecurity, jealousy, envy don't get much screen time. Instead Bollywood creates charming fairy tales of first-time romances, in which – mostly – the lovers live happily ever after. Love is shiningly pretty and achingly innocent. The key ingredients are fresh, easy-on-the-eye faces, foot-tapping music and beautiful locations. Every few years, a frothy love story, which blends these perfectly, becomes a box office rage and creates a new star. Many popular heroes – Sanjay Dutt, Aamir Khan, Hrithik Roshan, Bobby and Sunny Deol – have made their debuts with romances.

The plot is often propelled by disparity. Lovers must necessarily be divided. Destiny, wealth, family feuds, politics, caste, class, religion or even geography can play the villain. In the immensely successful *Ek Duje Ke Liye* (*Made for Each Other*, 1981), a Punjabi girl falls in love with a Tamil boy. Facing great opposition, they eventually commit suicide – if they can't live together, they decide they will die together. Love plumbs new heights as the odds against it mount. Passion and opposition are directly proportionate.

DDLJ followed the Bollywood romance rule book. But Aditya, reared on Hindi movies, tweaked every stereotype. By placing his characters abroad, he created new oppositions. The tired rich-boy–poor-girl conflict was replaced by a more understated but equally thorny issue: What constitutes Indianness, what makes us Hindustani? Raj and Simran are both Punjabi second-generation British Asians, but their romance is derailed by seemingly insurmountable odds because their worlds are shaped by differing definitions of 'Indian'. In its construction, *DDLJ* was familiar yet unique. From clichés, Aditya refashioned a contemporary blockbuster. He told a story that had been told many times before, but made it new.

Five

'Come ... Fall in Love'

DDLJ opens with Chaudhry Baldev Singh feeding pigeons in Trafalgar Square on a damp London morning. It's early and he is alone with the birds. His voice-over tells the audience that Baldev has lived in London for twenty-two years. Every day he walks this route to work and every day the street asks him his name. It asks him, 'Who are you, where are you from? Why are you here?' It is a poignant line that encapsulates Baldev's tragedy – after more than two decades, he is still an alien. Like the pigeons he feeds, Baldev is homeless.

Baldev is a man without a country. Financial constraints force him to live abroad – 'I am shackled to my bread,' he says – but his heart longs for the homeland he hasn't seen in two decades, Punjab. Watching the birds peck at grain, Baldev promises himself that some day he will return. The camera frames his face in a close-up. As it cuts to a wide shot, we see that Baldev has been transported back to Punjab. He is feeding pigeons in a lush field while singing girls run around him, trailing their brightly coloured dupattas. This blaze of sunshine and colour is in stark contrast to cold, alienating London. The girls sing to him:

Ghar aaja pardesi
Tera desh bulaye re

Come home, o wanderer,
Your land calls you

But the escape is momentary. Church bells bring Baldev back into the present, where he must walk to his convenience store and start the day. Baldev wasn't always this sombre and melancholy. In a scene that was edited out of the film, Simran asks her mother if her father ever smiled. Lajjo says that the sound of his laughter used to cross the river in Punjab. But a man called Narendra lured them abroad with the false promise of a job, and then robbed them, and since then Baldev's spirit has been smothered.

Lajjo, cheerful and chatty, is a contrast to Baldev. Bustling about the kitchen, she monitors her younger daughter Rajeshwari's breakfast, and fixes her school bag. Lajjo has not been embittered by their uprooting. She has focused her energies on her home and children. Unlike Baldev, Lajjo has made her peace with the new land.

While the rest of the family is busy with morning routines, Simran stands at her bedroom window, revelling in the breeze. Clearly she has no appointments to keep. Simran is a dreamer. She is a girl on the cusp of womanhood. Even the wind rustling her hair is sensual. Simran writes poetry about an unseen stranger who is teasing her in her dreams:

> *Uski sansen resham jaisi gaalon ko chhoo jati hain*
> *Uski haathon ki khushboo hai abtak mere balon mein*
> *Haan, aisa pehli baar hua hai satra-athra saalon mein*
> *Undekha, unjana koi aane laga khyalon mein*

> A silken breath brushes my cheeks
> My hair still smells of the fragrance on his hands

> Yes, it's happening for the first time in seventeen–eighteen years
> An unseen stranger is coming into my thoughts

Lajjo calls her bawli (mad) for dreaming about a man she hasn't met, but Simran is convinced that someone, somewhere is made for her.[58]

Simran sings to this unseen lover, asking him to face her. Freshly bathed, she scampers around her room in a towel, but her sensuality is playful and innocent, and not in the least experienced or worldly. As the song progresses, Simran prances around the house, jumping on sofas and kitchen cabinets as Lajjo keeps pace with an expression of affectionate exasperation. For the last refrain, Simran steps outside and sings in the rain.

The rain song, in which heroines invariably writhe in wet clothes, has long been used in Bollywood as a metaphor for sex. It is one way of getting around the strict Central Board for Film Certification (CBFC).[59] Director Raj Kapoor used it extensively – perhaps Bollywood's most notorious wet sari sequence is in Kapoor's *Ram Teri Ganga Maili* (*Ram Your Ganga Is Polluted,* 1985). Ganga, played by first-time actress Mandakini, bathes in a waterfall wearing only a white sari, which soaks through exposing her breasts. Yash was also an expert practitioner of the rain-song tactic.[60]

Aditya uses this vocabulary, but carefully softens the erotic sting. Despite her long residence in the heart of the decadent West, Simran is incandescently pure. Wearing a short white skirt and midriff-exposing blouse, she is sexual but also virginal. Her fantasy has a schoolgirl innocence. 'What do I do?' she sings. 'My heart yearns so.' While a soaked Simran longs for love, her mother hurriedly collects clothes from the washing line. Lajjo's presence tempers the tone. The song provides the viewer the pleasures of voyeurism, but adroitly steers clear of vulgarity, or of suggesting that Simran may actually engage in any un-Indian premarital sexual activity.

Simran's lover remains a mystery for her, but the audience sees him. The song's musical interludes introduce Raj. The first shot of him shows him scoring a try in a rough, rain-soaked rugby game. Raj is quite unlike Simran: she dreams, he does. A montage of shots establishes Raj – he swims and bowls expertly, and – incredibly enough – races a plane. Raj is wealthy, flashy and flirtatious. He picks up a sexy hitch-hiker. Later in the film, Raj flirts with consummate ease, using the same lines – 'Haven't we met before …? *Your* eyes remind me of someone' – first on Simran and then on her friend Sheena. Dressed in a leather jacket and riding a motorbike, Raj is the Indian incarnation of James Dean–style cool.[61]

In Indian films, 'Raj' is a popular name for romantic heroes. Aditya's inspiration was Raj Kapoor, who himself played heroes called Raj or Raju in his early classics, *Awara* (*The Vagabond*, 1951) and *Shri 420* (*Mr 420*, 1955). Later, when Kapoor directed the watershed teeny-bopper romance *Bobby* (1973), he named his hero Rajnath. In Aditya's screenplay for *DDLJ*, Raj's full name is Rajnath, but the full name is never used in the film. In another seminal love story, *Qayamat Se Qayamat Tak* (*From Eternity to Eternity*, 1988), Aamir Khan's character was also called Raj.

But unlike his predecessors, *DDLJ*'s Raj isn't the unblemished boy next door. He is resolutely irreverent and occasionally wicked. And though Aditya never spells it out, the film encourages us to feel that Raj is also sexually experienced. Originally, the scene in which Raj visits Baldev's store had him wanting to buy condoms. But later Aditya thought that condoms would be too much of a transgression, and so in the film, Raj wants only beer.

The subsequent scenes further establish the differences between Raj and Simran. He is playing the rich debauchee – drinking beer on a float in his pool – when he realizes that he is late for his graduation ceremony. He rushes to his university in a swanky Lamborghini, only to be declared the first student ever in the history of the institution to fail. Aditya had originally planned to intercut this scene with Simran winning the top honours at her college. Even Simran's food habits are conservative. Aditya's screenplay specifies that she is a vegetarian while Raj, ever the rogue, is willing to eat even a beef burger.

They live in the same city, but their worlds are separate and unalike. Simran is a middle-class girl. Her house is comfortable but frugal, especially compared to Raj's mansion, which features wall-to-wall carpeting, wood panelling and expensive objets d'arts. Baldev strives to preserve a little corner of Punjab in London. He wears only Indian clothes, as does Lajjo. At home, even the daughters are mostly in traditional Punjabi suits or salwar-kameezes. Baldev insists that the family participate in early morning prayers, even on Sundays.[62] He is an authoritarian who actively polices his children. In a short but insightful scene set in London, at the beginning of the film, Simran and Rajeshwari are shown dancing to Western pop music. Even Lajjo is doing a jig in the kitchen. But when the doorbell rings, the girls quickly change the music to an old Hindi film song by K.L. Saigal. They quickly sit on the sofa, pretending to read. They know Baldev wouldn't approve of them dancing to rock and roll. So they construct a secret life.

Raj doesn't need to keep any secrets. His father, Dharam Veer Malhotra, is the polar opposite of Baldev. Dharam Veer is garrulous and jovial, and is an indulgent parent. When Raj comes home with the news that he has failed at university, Dharam Veer laughs and pops open a bottle of champagne. Like a tour guide, he walks Raj down a wall of ancestral portraits, and explains how each one of his forefathers had also failed.[63]

Education has little value, Dharam Veer declares with a hearty laugh. He is proof of that: an uncouth tenth-standard dropout from dusty Bhatinda, he has become a millionaire in London through sheer hard work.

The debauched but inherently good-hearted Punjabi who loves and lives large has long been a fixture in Yash Chopra movies. In fact, Anupam Kher, who plays Dharam Veer, played a similar character in *Lamhe*. Prem is friend, philosopher and court jester for *Lamhe*'s hero Viren. But Dharam Veer's original avatar is Vijay Khanna in Yash's *Kabhi Kabhie*.[64] Vijay, who occasionally knocks back Scotch in the middle of the day, is flamboyant and loud. He is also his son Vicky's good friend. When Vicky falls in love, he calls his father to say: 'I'm in love, *yaar* (buddy).'

Later, when Vicky's fiancée leaves town, Vijay encourages him to go after her: *'Mard ke bachchhe bano. Pyar kiya hai to duniya ki had tak uska peecha karo'* (Be a man. If you love her, then pursue her to the ends of the earth). In *DDLJ*, Dharam Veer uses much the same macho logic on Raj once Simran has been spirited away to India by her father. *'Dulhan usiki hoti hai jo doli mein bithakar le aata hai. Maine tujhe tuntuna bajane ke liye payda nahin kiya tha ... ab ja aur is ghar mein tabhi aana jab bahu tere saath hogi'* (The bride goes to the man who brings her home. I didn't give you birth to sit around playing this fiddle ... Now go and come home only when your bride is with you).

Their camaraderie stands in contrast to the formal relationship Simran has with Baldev. The parent-as-friend model is clearly advocated by both Yash and Aditya in their films. In *Kabhi Kabhie*, the mother Pooja is also a 'buddy'. So Vicky gently ribs her about admirers she had in her college days, and they perform a gesture with their hands, accompanied by gibberish, which seals their special friendship. Raj and Dharam Veer also have a unique father–son ritual, which is used throughout the film. They sing out a nonsensical chant accompanied by hand gestures: *'O potchi, O koka, O bobi, O lola.'* Their physical comfort and spontaneity with each other is again quite different from the formal distance maintained between Simran and Baldev. Significantly, Simran calls Baldev 'Bauji' – a traditional and respectful way to address one's father – while Raj uses the more casual 'Pops' for Dharam Veer.

However, *DDLJ* isn't lazy in its characterizations. There are no obvious villains. Baldev isn't merely detestable and dictatorial; he is complex, and is driven by honourable intentions. In Aditya's original screenplay, there was a scene in which Baldev says to Simran, 'I know that I've brought you up like a tyrant but there is a reason for it. I have seen a lot of pain in life. I've seen people change and I never wanted my kids to come in touch with the people here. That's why I have protected you all.' Baldev is so afraid of losing his daughters to 'Angrezipan', westernization, that he cannot give them any breathing space. After a run-in with Raj at his shop, a furious Baldev calls westernized second-generation Indians a dhabba or blot on India. He compares them to the proverbial washerman's dog, who belongs neither to the ghar (house) nor the ghat (bathing or washing place on a riverbank). In reaction to the threat of corruption and destroying the culture of India, Baldev is necessarily a rigidly traditional father, so much so that he arranged Simran's marriage when she was a little girl, believing that it was the only way to protect her from the pollution of the West. And yet, when Simran seeks permission to go for a month-long holiday in Europe with her friends, Baldev agrees.

When Simran first asks to go on the Eurail, Lajjo laughs and suggests they call a doctor. Simran has obviously gone crazy. It seems impossible that Baldev would agree to his young, beautiful, single daughter travelling without a chaperone. And yet Simran puts it to him so artfully that he cannot say no. She says, 'I have never disobeyed you, Bauji. I'll be going away to a land I have never seen. The man I'm going to marry is a complete stranger. But I have no complaints. You must have considered my best interests. But I won't get a chance like this ever again. I don't know whether I'll ever come back here, whether I will have these friends later on. Besides, it's only a month. In a month, I will have lived a lifetime. For the sake of my happiness, won't you let me have a month of my life?'

Simran's appeal to borrow a month from her own life is heart-rending. Indeed, Simran's life is hardly her own. In Baldev's struggle to negotiate between tradition and modernity, Simran's desires as an individual have been completely negated. Till this day, she has been the virtuous, obedient daughter; and after marriage, she will be the virtuous, obedient wife. But she wants one month to be herself. In this one month, she will fulfil her dreams.

Baldev relents, but the ground rules don't change. A scene that was edited out of the film showed Baldev dropping Simran at the train station. Before leaving, he reminds her one more time that she is a Hindustani, an Indian. 'Don't do anything to shame my trust,' he says. And Simran replies that she is aware of only one thing, that she is Chaudhry Baldev Singh's daughter. That simple assertion contains an entire code of ethics, an entire world.

THE COURSE OF TRUE LOVE

Of course the father and daughter haven't counted on Raj. After establishing their parallel lives and the vast oppositions that will obstruct a relationship, Aditya puts Raj and Simran on a train together. As Simran scrambles to get on the train, Raj puts out his hand and pulls her in, and we see a close-up of their clasped hands. The shot is repeated again at the end when Raj pulls her up on another train – this one taking them away from the Punjab village and back to London and a life together. Raj alone can yank Simran out of her straitjacketed life. He literally pulls her into another world. He is the modern-day knight in shining armour who saves the princess from many dragons, including her own father and a dreary, loveless life with her dull fiancé, Kuljeet.

Unlike many Bollywood lovers, Raj and Simran don't fall in love at first sight. There are no shy, stolen glances or poetic realizations of love. Instead Raj flirts, mocks and teases. He picks up her bra that has fallen out when her suitcase opened and embarrasses her with it. They are stuck in the area between compartments, so he paraphrases a line from a popular romantic song from *Bobby,* singing, *'Hum tum ek dibbe mein bandh ho'* (You and I are shut in a box).

While Simran finds Raj's flirting irritating, her friend Sheena is quite willing to flirt back. Later, during the club sequence in Paris, Simran and her friends are getting bored with the tedious opera singing. When the men enter the room, Sheena says, 'Girls … *Dekho,* boys' (look, boys). The women check them out enthusiastically. There is no coyness or apology. When Simran tells Sheena not to call them to their table, Sheena says, 'Come on, Simran, grow up.' The interaction between the men and the women is casual and modern. The fact that they are interested in boys doesn't make them bad girls. It just means that the hormones are kicking in. The banter and flirting is youthful and for Hindi movies, quite revolutionary.

Sooraj Barjatya's *Maine Pyar Kiya* (*I Have Fallen in Love,* 1989) was one of the early films to show a girl and a boy progressing from friendship to love. To underline the relationship, the boy, Prem, even gave the girl Suman a baseball cap with 'FRIEND' written on it. But their interaction is curiously puritanical. Though Prem has been educated in America (his room is papered with posters of Samantha Fox and Michael Jackson), he is, as a buxom seductress says, 'old-fashioned'. So when Prem must apply medicine to Suman's sprained calf, he closes his eyes because her ankles are exposed. He cannot violate her, even with his gaze.

DDLJ has a more relaxed attitude towards sexuality. The laxity applies only to the men – Hindi movie heroines are nearly always virgins, and *DDLJ* is not the kind of film in which a transgression of that rule is possible, or even thinkable. But Raj and Simran discuss relationships without awkwardness. Raj tells her that while he's had many affairs, he's never fallen in love. Their interaction feels realistically spontaneous and natural; there is no melodrama. Raj is constantly ribbing Simran. At the end of the song *'Rukh ja',* he abruptly drops her on the floor. He makes her miss the train and even manages to tear her blouse by mistake. Again there is a glimpse of a bra, but the scene is comical, not sensual.

This is of course a strictly sanitized view of the lives of second-generation NRIs. Other films like Stephen Frears's *My Beautiful Laundrette* (1985) and Srinivas Krishna's *Masala* (1991) have painted more searing portraits of immigrant life. In these films, the characters are homosexuals or heroin addicts, and sometimes indulge in sexual pranks out of plain boredom. In *Laundrette,* a Pakistani girl flashes her breasts at a party just for a lark. But *DDLJ* acknowledges none of the angst of being outsiders. Raj, Simran and their friends are improbably wholesome and uncomplicated. The outside universe doesn't impinge on them. Sex, drugs and alcohol haven't touched their lives. The worst thing Raj can do is spray water at Simran with a trick flower.

In this carefully constructed, sunlit world, love is destined. Early in the film, Simran and Raj pass each other on a street. Both are talking to their own friends about the upcoming Eurail trip. When they pass, the film shifts to slow motion, freezing the moment. Aditya skilfully teases the viewers, who know that in the coming scenes these strangers will fall in love.[65] Later, when Raj is talking to Simran about his dream lover, his words echo her poetry. He too speaks of an unseen stranger who calls him from behind the clouds. Despite their differences, Raj and Simran speak the same language. They also, as it turns out, share the same values.

DDLJ is full of small surprises. Aditya expertly reverses scenes so they end in new places. A morning-after sequence begins on a comic note and ends with Raj and Simran becoming emotionally intimate. Raj and Simran spend a night in the same bed, but it is not the night but the morning that changes their relationship, and our understanding of Raj. Aditya uses an old movie ploy to get Raj and Simran in bed – on a bitterly cold night, she drinks cognac – but the scenes that follow are far from hackneyed.[66]

Quite intoxicated after the cognac, Simran seems to break free from the shackles of being Chaudhry Baldev Singh's daughter. She runs down the street, wears a short, red miniskirt in the snow, and sings suggestively:

Thandi thandi pavan
Jalta hai yeh badan

Jee chahta hai banalun
Tujhko apna sajan

The breeze is cool
But my body burns
My heart desires
That I should make you my lover

Raj declines the invitation. He changes Simran out of her wet clothes, but goes no further. The next morning, Raj fools Simran into believing that they have made love, but when she breaks down crying, he says, 'I know what you think of me. You think I'm a wastrel. But I'm not scum, Simran. I'm a Hindustani and I know what honour means for the Hindustani woman. Not even in my dreams can I imagine doing that to you.'

Baldev defines Indian in the narrow, obvious way – through his clothes, his daily rituals and his strict surveillance of his two daughters and wife. Raj expands the definition. He is unkempt, cocky and even a badmash (scoundrel), but his heart is Hindustani. As Raj Kapoor sang in *Shri 420:*

Mera joota hai Japani
Yeh patloon Englishtani

Sar pe lal topi Rusi
Phir bhi dil hai Hindustani[67]

My shoes are Japanese
These pants are British
The cap on my head is Russian
But my heart is Indian

What makes an Indian a true Indian is not the externals. It's the dil (heart) that counts. Later in the film, Dharam Veer tells Baldev not to be fooled by his Western clothes – Dharam Veer almost always wears spiffy pants and cravats – because he carries India in his heart. Indian values are portable and malleable. The man in the Harley-Davidson leather jacket can be as Hindustani as the man in the dhoti-kurta.

A few scenes after the morning-after sequence, Raj reiterates that he may have been brought up in England but he is Hindustani. The film has by now shifted to Punjab, through a couple of adroit sidesteps past logic. Baldev, furious that Simran has broken his trust by falling in love, somehow sells his business overnight and moves to Punjab, where Raj somehow traces them despite not knowing their address. But Raj and Simran's reunion in a field of swaying yellow mustard is a superb cinematic high. Simran, hearing Raj's mandolin, runs out into the field. The sound has been haunting her but this time the music is real. She sees a cow wearing a Swiss cowbell and then Raj.

In Aditya's first draft, Simran asks Raj, 'What are you doing here?' He replies, 'Do I still have to word it [sic] – 1 love you dammit [sic]. I can't live without you. Be mine forever.' But later, Aditya decides to do away with dialogue. Instead, the heightened emotions are encapsulated in a song. Raj sings:

Tujhe dekha to yeh jana sanam
Pyar hota hai deewana sanam

Since I saw you, I realized
What madness love is

He opens his arms, and Simran – dressed in virginal white – runs into them. In the musical interludes, the lovers fantasize about revisiting all the places they have seen in Europe, but this time as a married couple. In this sequence, Aditya borrows liberally from his father's filmic vocabulary. Simran, wearing a diaphanous sari, sings with Raj on snow-covered Swiss mountains. The mustard field is a

Hindustani version of the blooming tulip gardens in Yash's *Silsila*.⁶⁸

When the song is over, Simran's first words to Raj are, 'Take me away from here.' In her mind there is no option but to elope. Love has altered the obedient girl. She is now willing to rebel. *DDLJ* is influenced by Sooraj Barjatya's cinema, but Aditya's heroine is different in her willingness to defy the system. Barjatya's women are unusually compliant – the simpering Suman in *Maine Pyar Kiya* certainly is. Nisha in Barjatya's *Hum Aapke Hain Koun...?* is a college graduate, but she meekly agrees to marry her widowed brother-in-law so that she can look after his newborn child. Unlike them, Simran has spunk.

A Moral Twist

But Raj refuses to elope. This is *DDLJ*'s grand twist. Rebellion is part of Bollywood's formula for cinematic romance. Every decade has a defining love story, in which at some point the lovers confront their parents. In the classic *Mughal-e-Azam* (*The Mughal Emperor*, 1960), a quasi-historical epic, Prince Salim takes an army against his father, Emperor Akbar, because Akbar disapproves of his affair with a mere palace dancer. Salim is defeated and sentenced to death by his father. He survives but the object of his desire, Anarkali, is entombed alive in a wall. Later generations chose the easier option of running away. In Kapoor's blockbuster *Bobby*, just before he elopes, the eighteen-year-old hero Raj asks his cold businessman father: *'Yeh meri zindagi hai, iska faisla karnewale aap kaun hote hain?'* (This is my life. Who are you to make decisions for me?).

Fifteen years later, another Raj in *Qayamat Se Qayamat Tak*, tells his girlfriend Rashmi, 'The authority to make a decision regarding my life and your life is neither with your father, nor with my father. We are their children but not their property.' Raja in *Dil* (*Heart*, 1990) goes one step further. When the father of his beloved refuses to relent, he storms into Madhu's house, locks himself and her inside a room, breaks a wooden stool, sets it on fire, and then, while her father watches through a grilled window, takes the seven sacred pheras (circles) around the fire. To seal this unconventional marriage, he cuts his finger and fills the parting in Madhu's hair with blood as a substitute for sindoor, the vermillion powder that married Hindu women wear in their hair.

Many lovers run away (often on motorcycles) and then set up home in pastoral surroundings. In *Love Story* (1981), Bunty and his sixteen-year-old amour escape to a valley of flowers, where they build a wooden house. The house has a thatched roof, curtains and even the nameplate 'Bunty and Pinky'. He finds a job as a woodcutter in the nearby village, while she cooks and cleans. Of course despite sharing a home, they never share a bed. She sleeps in a hammock, and he on the floor. They are not two adults in a relationship but children playing house.

In *DDLJ*, Raj's dissent is unique. He rebels by refusing to do so. Raj tells Simran, *'Main tumhe bhagakar ya churakar le jane nahin aaye hun. Bhale meri paydaish* England *mein hui ho par hun main Hindustani. Main yahan tumhe apni dulhan banane ke liye aaya hun aur tumhe yahan se le jaoonga tabhi jab tumhare bauji khud tumhara haath mere haath mein denge.'* (I haven't come here to elope with you or to steal you. I might be born in England but I am Hindustani. I've come here to make you my bride. I'll take you from here only when your Bauji gives me your hand in marriage.)

In later scenes, both Lajjo and Dharam Veer

separately suggest to Raj that he should run away with Simran. In a poignant sequence, Lajjo gives Simran her jewellery – the only thing she owns – and tells them to leave. But Raj refuses. There are always two roads, he tells Lajjo, the right one and the wrong one. And though the wrong route is seductive in its ease, he will take the more difficult, correct path. Because, he says, he doesn't want to snatch or steal Simran. He wants to marry her with the approval of the family.

In Raj Kapoor's *Prem Rog* (*Lovesickness,* 1982), a feudal drama about the forbidden remarriage of a widow, a landowner's widowed daughter falls in love with her childhood friend. Rather than face the ignominy of his daughter remarrying, Thakur suggests that the boy Dev run away with her. But Dev refuses saying that the battle is a dharam yudh or moral war, in which there can be no compromises. For Raj too, marrying Simran becomes a dharam yudh. He believes that their love will conquer all opposition.

Raj's decision echoes also Yash's lovers in *Kabhi Kabhie*. In that film, when Pooja's parents arrange her marriage to another man, Amit decides that they must not defy them. He says, *'Humen koi hak nahin pahunchta hai ki hum apni khushi ke liye apne ma-baap ke armanon ka gala ghot de, unki lashon par apne pyar ka mahal banaye*'[69] (We have no right to strangle the wishes of our parents for our own happiness, and create our palace of love on top of their corpse).

Amit, the brooding poet, watches silently from afar as his beloved is married off. Raj, the modern-day yuppie, has no such plans. Instead, like a CEO (chief executive officer) taking over a rival company through strategy and unbreakable resolve, Raj takes over Simran's family, one by one.[70]

Under the disguise of a prospective investor looking for land, Raj ingratiates himself to both Simran and Kuljeet's families. Like Barjatya's *Hum Aapke Hain Koun…?*, *DDLJ* also portrays the great, undivided Indian family. In London, the family is a nuclear unit, while in Punjab the family is extended to include relatives and neighbours. But there is no dysfunction or dissension. All the members are cheerful and in harmony with themselves and their place in this world. The women do kitchen work and serve food while the men chat and play chess. It is unclear whether anyone is gainfully employed. The homes are comfortable but not lavish. It is a utopian world, perhaps less cloyingly sugar-coated than Barjatya's, but perfect all the same.

During the flurry of wedding festivities, Raj starts to make inroads into the family. He charms each of the members of Simran's extended family, one by one. Aditya creates a typical Punjabi wedding atmosphere with near-constant gana-bajana (singing) and chai-pani (light refreshments). Here too the film resembles *Hum Aapke Hain Koun...?*, but more than Barjatya, Aditya is following in his father's footsteps. Yash was the original wedding specialist. The extravagant Punjabi wedding, which found an international audience with Mira Nair's *Monsoon Wedding* (2001), first featured in Yash's films.

In *Kabhi Kabhie*, the titles roll on a wedding sequence – women play the dholak (drum) and dance while the bride waits on the nuptial bed, her head lowered and her lips trembling. In *Silsila*, the lovers first meet at a marriage and through a song, flirt with each other. In *Chandni*, the first half of the film is almost entirely devoted to wedding ceremonies. The lovers meet and court over the several days that the wedding lasts. Later, at their own engagement, both sing and dance. The wedding songs in Yash's films are often sung by his wife Pamela. Aditya also followed suit. *'Ghar aaja pardesi'* (Come home wanderer), a folksy number which is also used during the wedding rituals in *DDLJ*, features Pamela's voice.

In *DDLJ*, during the course of a conventional wedding, Raj becomes the unconventional element. He enters as Kuljeet's friend, but quickly switches allegiances to Simran's side. So he takes a tray of sweets from Lajjo's hand and starts serving the guests. At most Indian weddings, the bride and the groom are not equals. In an insightful scene in director Raj Kumar Santoshi's *Lajja* (*Shame*, 2001), two runaways gatecrash a wedding. The man tells the woman how to identify the bride's father: he is the man whose back is bent over from bowing deferentially to everyone. Though both giving and taking dowry is illegal in India, monetary exchange is routine, especially in certain communities. After the wedding, continued harassment of the bride for money and even murder is not uncommon.

Given these grim realities (which of course never intrude in *DDLJ*), Raj's behaviour is radical. In later scenes, he helps Baldev's younger sister pick an appropriate sari, serves drinks and brings bushels of grain to the kitchen. Raj is the only male to enter these female spaces. He sits in the kitchen and peels carrots while he talks. In a scene that was deleted, Raj sits in the kitchen surrounded by the ladies of the house. He is narrating the story of two nameless lovers who are thwarted by the girl's stubborn father. The women hang on to every word and the unmarried aunt, carried away by the drama, even holds his hand.

MEN AND WOMEN

DDLJ presents Raj as the ideal Indian male. While the other men – Baldev, Kuljeet – are sometimes boorish and blatantly chauvinistic, Raj is the perfect blend of the modern and the traditional. He is progressive in certain situations and rigidly conservative in others. He plays by the rules but he also tweaks them. When Simran decides to keep Karva Chauth, Raj supports her. Karva Chauth is a largely north Indian ritual in which married Hindu women keep a day-long fast, abstaining from food and water, for the prosperity and longevity of their husbands. Feminists have long railed against this gendered practice (married Hindu men are not required to observe a similar fast) but the ritual continues to be immensely popular. With the sudden deluge of large Hindu families in films and television, Karva Chauth is also getting more screen time.[71]

Aditya, who grew up watching his mother do Karva Chauth, puts a modern twist on it. Simran, the bride-to-be, decides to fast for her future husband. In her mind, of course, that is Raj and not Kuljeet. Raj doesn't take the ritual too seriously – when Simran complains of hunger pangs, he tries to sneak her a ladoo. But as a token of his love and solidarity, Raj also fasts. Karva Chauth ends with the ritual viewing of the rising moon by the fasting couple. On the moonlit terrace, away from the prying eyes of the family, Raj and Simran break their fast together. Aditya had originally planned to do an elaborate song sequence in which Raj keeps the starving women entertained by impersonating each person in the family. The women sing: *'O Angrezi babu, kahan se aaya tu?'* (O English babu, where have you come from?)[72] In his participation in these female rituals, and in his easy movement through spaces inhabited by women, Raj is quite unlike most Hindi film heroes, and especially unlike the macho angry young men who dominated the cinema in the 1970s and 1980s.

But Raj is equally adept at being one of the boys. He knocks back beer with Kuljeet and shows Baldev some nifty chess moves. Raj and Baldev bond over early morning pigeon-feeding sessions. The serenity of the surroundings aids Raj's cause. Baldev slowly warms to the boy. Raj makes Baldev's beloved pigeons a metaphor for himself and the millions of Indians who migrate. When Baldev says that in London even the pigeons seem strangers, Raj points out that perhaps their unfamiliarity is in Baldev's perspective. Perhaps one of the pigeons he fed in Trafalgar Square had flown there from Punjab. Indeed, Raj may seem alien, but a slight shift of focus will reveal that he is as Hindustani as Baldev. As they talk, a pigeon comes crashing to the ground. Kuljeet, ostensibly the native Punjab da puttar (son of Punjab), is hunting. And Raj, ostensibly the 'foreigner', picks the bird up and heals it by putting matti (earth) on the wound. Raj literally proves himself to be a son of the soil.

Kuljeet is a lout. In a scene with Dharam Veer, he suggests with macho bravado that after his marriage, he will come to London to check out the mema-shemas (English babes). Yet Baldev mistakenly believes him to be the perfect match for

Simran. In a scene that was deleted, Lajjo pleads with Baldev to at least ask Simran about the man she loves. He refuses, saying that any boy who is not familiar with Indian culture cannot make Simran happy. The irony for the viewer is that Kuljeet, born and bred in Punjab, is 'un-Indian', while Raj, born and bred in London, is 'Indian'. Baldev is furious that Lajjo is questioning his judgement. He genuinely believes that he is acting in Simran's best interests.

In this patriarchal world, women have little power. Simran's life is steered first by Baldev and then by Raj. The men decide the course of action, and the women, the repository of Hindustani culture and values, toe the line. This is not unusual. Hindi films and the Hindi film industry are hero-centric, patriarchal. Most mainstream films use heroines as visual distractions. They are trendily dressed stereotypes. The supporting female characters are usually also variations of clichés – the benevolent mother, the scheming daughter-in-law, the wicked stepmother or the victim sister who gets raped/killed/sold. *DDLJ* operates very much within this male matrix of power and honour. Simran is an amaanat (property) to be passed from Baldev to

Raj. But the film is distinctive in that it fleshes out its female characters, and it at least records these dissenting voices. Lajjo and Simran are keenly aware of their position.

Their relationship is finely etched. The first scene between them establishes that Simran shares a special closeness with Lajjo. Lajjo reads Simran's moony poetry without judgement. She tells her that when a daughter grows up, the mother isn't a mother any more but a friend. She is also sensitive to Simran's predicament. In one scene, Simran is reading aloud to the family a letter from Kuljeet's father to Baldev. But when she comes to lines about her impending marriage to Kuljeet, she stops and leaves the room. Baldev is ecstatic because he thinks she is feeling shy – a sure sign that he has brought her up well. But Lajjo knows better – she knows that Simran is upset. Later, she gently comforts Simran, saying that perhaps Kuljeet will be the unseen stranger Simran is looking for.

In one of the best-written scenes in *DDLJ*, Lajjo asks Simran to forget Raj. Lajjo tearfully draws on her own life: her father had always told her that there is no difference between men and women, but when she grew up she discovered that this was a lie. Her education was stopped so that her brothers could study, and since then she has continued to make sacrifices in different guises – as daughter, sister and wife. Lajjo's poignant words resonate with the experience of millions of Indian women. When her daughters were born, Lajjo had resolved that their lives would be different. But she was mistaken. Lajjo says, *'Beti, isliye aaj main, teri ma, tujhse teri khushiyan maangne aayee hu. Tu usse bhool ja beti'* (Therefore I, your mother, have come to ask from you, your happiness. Forget him, my child). Simran agrees to forget Raj, and they hold each other and cry.

The women instinctively know each other's pain, which men are unable to see. In one scene, Simran's grandmother asks Baldev why Simran's eyes are sad and her laughter so hesitant. Baldev attributes it to the new place and new people and asks her not to worry unnecessarily. But his mother knows that something is amiss. Women are also more insightful. Even the twelve-year-old Rajeshwari can see through Kuljeet – she turns up her nose at him at first sight. Lajjo tries to help Simran break out of the patriarchal prison they both live in. She actively encourages her to run away. At the end of the film, she takes Simran to the station where Raj is waiting. But only Baldev has the final authority to give his daughter away.

DDLJ recognizes the inequity between men and women but affirms the status quo. Like Barjatya's *Hum Aapke Hain Koun...?*, it establishes the importance of the family over the individual. The family is what makes Indian culture unique, and the family – in this telling – is the jagir or property of men. The road to happiness lies in preserving this structure of ownership and power, not rebelling against it. When Baldev discovers the truth, he slaps Raj, not once but eight times. Simran, weeping, tells him they should have run away. But Raj refuses this assertion. 'Where can you run from your own people?' he says. 'Our parents have raised us with love and can decide for us better than we can.'

Raj's words are a startling contrast to the speeches lovers usually make at such juncture in the plot. In *Bobby*, just before the lovers take a despairing, suicidal leap off a cliff into rushing water, Raj tells his father, *'Hum aapke bachche zaroor hain, magar aapki zaydaat nahin'* (We are your children, but we are not your property).

DDLJ's Raj insists that the opposite is true, that children are indeed the property of their parents, and that women are the property of men. Parental approval is critical for love to thrive. A love marriage must also be arranged. Raj's conviction triumphs in the end. Finally, Baldev gives away his amaanat to Raj. Faced by the truth that Raj has not run away with Simran, that he has acted like a 'true' Hindustani (despite his duplicitous entry into Simran's wedding), Baldev relents. He lets loose his firm grip on Simran's hand, and she runs towards Raj. Their hands join. The brave heart eventually wins the bride.

Six

Tradition and Modernity, Fear and Comfort

DDLJ was a fortuitous meeting of talent and timing. In a complicated age, it offered uncomplicated solutions. In the 1990s, India underwent vertiginous rushes of change. Children interacted with foreign cultures and values as never before, and some of them put on Harley-Davidson jackets and affected a language of cool that was incomprehensible to their parents. The family faced the added pressures of both parents having to work, of the dissatisfactions of women and their desire for autonomy, of divorce.

Sexuality was pulled out from its musty Indian closet. There was a proliferation of sleek, semi-clad bodies: magazines (even 'respectable' ones like *Filmfare* and *Femina*), music videos and films pushed the limits of what was acceptable. Middle-class Indians were seen discussing their kinks and longings in print and on television.[73] Television soaps, watched by housewives across India, told stories of premarital sex and adultery.[74] Indians now seemed to be willing to recognize – at least on the small screen and in the print media – that they were having sex, and that much of it was not of the married variety. Certainly, a generation of urban teenagers in the great metropolitan cities of Mumbai, Delhi and Kolkata engaged in sexual activity with the same gusto that their counterparts in New York or Paris might.[75]

All of these movements and shifts were paralleled by the rise of various fundamentalisms, in particular the rise of a muscular Hindu right wing, which has attempted to define 'Indian culture' in particularly narrow terms. The debate over what is properly Indian and what constitutes a foreign invasion or neo-colonialism has been a constant feature of public discourse in recent years. Much of this debate has been focused on women and their bodies, on what constitutes a Bhartiya nari or virtuous Indian woman.

The nation state of India itself is often incarnated as Bharat Mata, or Mother India, who is usually white-clad and quite completely virtuous. Politicians often tell the populace that the virtue and honour of Bharat Mata must be protected. This modern Bharat Mata is quite unlike other, older goddesses from the Hindu pantheon, many of whom are quite unambiguously sexual and autonomous in their actions. They are independent beings, and are sometimes terrifying in their power. They need no protection, and in fact are often the ones who protect the male gods from some demon or other.

The conflict in *DDLJ* hinges on Simran, on what is to be her fate. The film presents a poignant understanding of the frustrations and longings of its female characters. But it determinedly and artfully refuses to accord Simran any agency, any ability to act on her own. After her first impulse to run away, she waits quietly for the struggle between her father and her lover to decide her fortunes, and at the end is released from one male to the custody of another. In the second half of the film, she becomes curiously still; the camera often finds her sitting, not moving, as the wedding and the machinations of Raj whirl about her. She becomes increasingly passive as the story unfolds. And she remains, to the end of the film, virginal.

The conversation between tradition and modernity in India (and in London) is an ongoing one. Indians do not want to jettison the past altogether, and they do want the modern, the new; they are creative in their techniques for combining the two, but the process is not without pain, failure and loss. The real-life versions of Raj and Simran engage in this struggle every day, and they create new solutions and compromises to deal with these questions of autonomy, sexuality and selfhood. Indians are of course Indian in many different ways; a nation of a billion people, which holds together dozens of languages and dozens of ethnicities and cultures, cannot hold to any simple and narrow definition of national character. As *DDLJ* recognizes, an Indian in a Harley-Davidson jacket can be as Indian as one in a dhoti. As the song has it, it is the dil (heart) that counts, not the Japanese shoes. But the dil that faces these questions must indeed be brave, capable of enormous generosity and enormous change, even as it maintains its own integrity.

DDLJ deals with these urgent questions, and the answers it offers are startlingly conservative, especially in its notions of what a woman should want, or expect. The film's Simran is a Bhartiya nari who does not threaten anyone, least of all the structures that keep her firmly in her place. The film seems to suggest that these great struggles of redefinition – of Indianness, of individual selves, of the nation state – can and will be easily resolved if women are properly controlled, if their sexuality is constrained. The paradox, of course, is that Indian women are now more unwilling than ever to be controlled or constrained.[76]

And that, perhaps, is the great comfort that *DDLJ* offers. It offers, to both men and women, to everyone who faces the terrifying uncertainties of new freedoms and the unpredictable future, a vision of a present which combines both the stability of the old order and the enticing choices of the new. *DDLJ* fills us with a nostalgia for a possible present in which Baldev and Raj and Simran and Lajjo can exist together without anyone's feelings being irretrievably hurt, without any hearts being broken, without any ruptures or bloodshed, and – especially – without anyone having unsanctioned sex.

That this golden present does not exist is precisely beside the point. The cinema of Aditya Chopra, and his fellow directors, Sooraj Barjatya and Karan Johar, presents life not as it is, but as it should be. Indian films are routinely accused of being 'escapist', but many Indian song-and-dance movies present a gritty reality full of violence, corruption and despair. But *DDLJ* and other films like it create a shining, perfect world that edits out heat, dust, crows, crowded streets.

These films delight in extraordinary riches, in beautiful and huge sets, in foreign locations; they are sometimes described as 'epic'. They are 'epic' in the most cursory sense, in that they create larger-than-life characters who exist in idealized landscapes; but these films carefully avoid those essential aspects of the epic, that profound sense of tragedy and the shattering spectacle of individuals being overwhelmed by time and circumstances. Despite their magical motifs, the great old stories were realistic in the most unrelenting way. But the new generation of neo-conservative film-makers are not interested in that kind of epic realism. They offer the comfortable, fluffy belief – if only for a few hours – that all is well with India, and the world. And this, perhaps, is a belief we need right now, especially in India.

The irony is that these films are being made by young and intelligent men who are fully conversant with the reality of the streets that they have grown up in and with the complexities – social and sexual – of the lives they themselves lead. Prior generations of Hindi film directors made films that questioned at least some aspects of the status quo, that were critical of the political system, of the second-class status of women, of society at large. Some even grappled with issues of sexuality. Many of Yash Chopra's early films like *Dhool ka Phool, Kabhi Kabhie* and *Trishul* (*Trident*, 1978) featured illegitimate children as protagonists. But in the dizzying climate of the 1990s, a slew of film-makers seemed to want to return to an India that never was. Perhaps this is exactly why their films are so successful.

At least on the large screen, within the ritual space of the cinema, Indian audiences all over the world seem to want a representation of culture and change that is warmly reassuring, soothing. In particular, Indian actresses are asked to portray virtuous Bhartiya naris on the screen. The irony is that popular film gossip magazines like *Stardust* regularly carry long articles about the deliciously unvirtuous activities of the members of the film industry, female and male. The readers of these magazines, across India and the globe, lead lives that are as messy and complicated as the lives of the 'filmi types' they read avidly about. At least for now, these readers are quite willing to pay terah ka tees, thirty rupees for a thirteen-rupee ticket, to participate in an enactment of simplicity. This is not quite 'escapism' – reality never goes away completely, not in an Indian theatre – but it is a necessary comfort, and a collective expression of hope. Besides, all of it is enormous fun.

Finally, however, no post-mortem can sufficiently explain why *DDLJ* still draws an audience, after so many years. It is a masterfully made film, which brings together a brilliant director with a talented cast. Its scenes are surprising and fresh, and the film is poignant, affecting and entertaining. The director of *DDLJ* is cinematically literate in the language of Indian movies, and uses the tropes of this cinema in a sophisticated and creative fashion. Aditya's education in Indian cinema started as soon as he was able to see and listen, and in *DDLJ* he has shown himself to be an adept heir to his father and this entire tradition.

Shah Rukh Khan believes that *DDLJ*'s 'magic' cannot be analysed. On a poster of *DDLJ* that hangs in Aditya's office, Shah Rukh has scribbled:

> Dear Adi,
> More than half my career ago, you gave me a dream to cherish all my life.
>
> My kids will see it, my grand children will love it and I'm sure even in heaven they are playing our film – so my parents would have seen it too. Thanx for taking me to them and making me the star I'm today. Lots of love and come let's make some more dreams together,
> God bless,
> Shah Rukh

Years later, *DDLJ* is still inviting people to 'Come ... fall in love.'

Notes

1. The Federation of Indian Chambers of Commerce and Industry (FICCI), *Indian Entertainment Industry,* March 2002, p. 11.
2. Nasreen Munni Kabir, *Bollywood: The Indian Cinema Story* (London: Channel 4 Books, 2001), p. 1.
3. When blockbuster *Kabhi Khushi Kabhie Gham* (*Sometimes Happiness, Sometimes Sadness*) was released in December 2001, the Bollywood grapevine was agog with rumours that the black market ticket prices had touched 1,000 rupees.
4. Since 1996, *DDLJ* has been officially telecast twice every year. But piracy is rampant in India and there is no way to estimate the unofficial screenings on the various cable and satellite channels.
5. In 2001, 230 Hindi films were released, averaging four a week.

6. Since *DDLJ* won the 1995 National Award for 'Wholesome Entertainment', it is exempted from entertainment tax. Ticket prices have been slashed to less than half of the regular price – tickets sell for nine rupees for the stalls and thirteen rupees for the balcony.
7. Despite being the largest film producer in the world, the Indian film industry remains an informal, amorphous business where many transactions are in unreported 'black' money. Therefore trade figures are not exact but estimates.
8. This is an average. In 2001, 1,013 films were produced. Since 1931, when talkies were introduced, India has produced more than 67,000 films in thirty languages.
9. FICCI, *Indian Entertainment Industry*, p. 11.
10. Some films are longer: *Mera Naam Joker* (*My Name Is Joker*, 1970) runs for four hours and fifteen minutes; *Mohabbatein* (*Loves*, 2000) for three hours and thirty-six minutes; *Lagaan* (*Land Tax*, 2001) for three hours and forty-two minutes. The length of Bollywood films makes it necessary to have an interval.
11. Ashis Nandy (ed.), *The Secret Politics of Our Desires: Innocence, Culpability and Popular Cinema* (New Delhi: Oxford University Press, 1998), p. 7.
12. Trade sources peg the annual success to failure ratio

at 20:80; but in the last few years, the successes have dipped even lower.
13. The publicity promised that *Sangam* was 'Ageless as Asia' and 'Exciting as Europe'.
14. Yash had shot in the Swiss village of Rossiniere so much that a local lake is unofficially called the Chopra Lake.
15. Except *Lamhe*, which had an NRI hero and much of the film's second half was shot abroad.
16. Punjab, or the land of five rivers, is a primarily agricultural state in northern India. The Punjabis are typically regarded as rich, robust and earthy.
17. The film, estimated to have taken over 700 million rupees across India, is one of the biggest hits ever in Hindi cinema.
18. In Mumbai's Liberty theatre, the best seats – in the dress circle – were upped from fifty rupees to seventy-five rupees and eventually to 100 rupees at the weekend.
19. Saibal Chatterjee, 'Back to the Movies', *Outlook,* 17 January 1996, pp. 58–63.
20. Anupama Chandra, 'Goodbye to Formula?', *India Today,* 30 November 1995, pp. 184–87.
21. This was an educated guess based on trade trends. Unlike Hollywood, the Hindi film industry rarely conducts any studies on audience demographics and behaviour.

22. Anupama Chopra, 'Candy Floss Films', *India Today*, 9 February 1998, pp. 78–79.
23. Anupama Chopra, 'Golden Goose', *India Today*, 1 November 1999, pp. 99–100.
24. This, however, was no indication of his future. Farhan's debut film *Dil Chahta Hai* (*The Heart Desires*, 2001) won both critical acclaim and commercial success.
25. Rachel Dwyer, *Yash Chopra* (London: BFI, 2002), p. x.
26. The 1950s are considered the golden era when filmmakers like Raj Kapoor, Bimal Roy, Mehboob Khan and Guru Dutt were at the peak of their talents.
27. Aditya sat for all his exams and did get a BCom degree but it is still lying uncollected at the University of Bombay.
28. Aditya stuck to the mainstream. To date he hasn't seen a single Satyajit Ray movie. He owns Ray's classic *Pather Panchali* (*Song of the Road*, 1955) but it lies in his room, unviewed.
29. Success hasn't broken this habit. He still watches almost every film on the day of release in a theatre.
30. Aditya maintains that *Lamhe*'s failure has gone a long way in grounding him. He will never get carried away by his successes because he knows how easily movies can go wrong.
31. It didn't help. *Parampara* flopped immediately.

32. *Mohabbatein* became his second film.
33. In Karan Johar's second film, *Kabhi Khushi Kabhie Gham,* Hrithik Roshan's child avatar, a plump snob, is autobiographical.
34. Uday's dream was fulfilled with Aditya's second film, *Mohabbatein,* in which he is one of the leads.
35. Eventually Aditya didn't do any shooting in Southall because of crowd-control problems.
36. Kajol's grandmother Shobhana Samarth, her mother Tanuja and her aunt Nutan were all leading actresses.
37. A slew of films, with titles taken from popular film songs, followed *DDLJ.*
38. Rachel Dwyer, *Yash Chopra,* p. 3.
39. Anand, much in demand until his death on 30 March 2002, wrote a total of approximately 4,000 songs.
40. Leading stars like Aamir Khan and Shah Rukh have understood the value of shooting one film at a stretch, and have greatly streamlined their work. Aamir does three films in a year. This is a sea change from the 1970s when a star like Shashi Kapoor once shot for three films simultaneously at the same studio. Shashi was called the 'taxi' star because he was constantly running from one studio to the next.
41. There have been exceptions: the Oscar-nominated *Lagaan* and Farhan Akhtar's *Dil Chahta Hai* were mostly done in synch sound.

42. The Shah Rukh–Kajol chemistry has endured through the decade with hits like *Kuch Kuch Hota Hai* and *Kabhi Khushi Kabhie Gham*. In January 2002, they were awarded the 'Asian Paints Jodi Number One Most Memorable Screen Pair' award at the Screen Awards. Shah Rukh says: 'We've been seen so much that now the director no longer has to work hard to show that we are in love. In *Kabhi Khushi,* we come on screen and we are in love. The audience accepts the pair. It's like that.'
43. Looking back now, Aditya feels that the costumes weren't up to the mark, and if he had to remake the film, he would add a lot more glamour.
44. In appreciation, Karan presented Farah with two pairs of garter socks.
45. Like Memorial Day in Hollywood, Diwali is considered to be a bumper box office period for Hindi movies.
46. Later, Aditya took off another one-and-a-half minutes. *DDLJ*'s final length is three hours and ten minutes.
47. D.G. Phalke, maker of the first Indian film *Raja Harishchandra* (1913), made a one-reel short called *How Films Are Prepared* about its making.
48. The record remained unequalled till Sanjay Leela Bhansali's *Black* won eleven awards in 2006.
49. This aspect of Aditya did not rub off on Karan,

who is extremely media-friendly. Karan is now widely recognized by crowds and so he rarely joins Aditya on his first-day–first-show outings.
50. Ashis Nandy (ed.), *The Secret Politics of Our Desires,* p. 4.
51. Pavan K. Varma, *The Great Indian Middle Class* (New Delhi: Penguin India, 1999), p. 167.
52. Ibid., p. 169.
53. A sampling of titles of stories carried in *India Today:* 'Suicides: A Growing Death Wish' (30 June 1996), 'Disturbed Generation' (24 November 1997), 'Stress Management' (9 June 1997), 'Marriage: Till Whims Do Us Part' (3 August 1998).
54. Patricia Uberoi, 'Imagining the Family: An Ethnography of Viewing *Hum Aapke Hain Koun...?*', in *Pleasure and the Nation,* ed. by Rachel Dwyer and Christopher Pinney (New Delhi: Oxford University Press, 2001), p. 336.
55. Patricia Uberoi, 'The Diaspora Comes Home: Disciplining Desire in *DDLJ*', *Contributions to Indian Sociology,* Vol. 32, No. 2, July–December 1998, p. 334.
56. Rachel Dwyer, *All You Want Is Money, All You Need Is Love* (London: Cassell, 2000), p. 150.
57. Madhu Jain and Nandita Chowdhury, 'Coming Home', *India Today,* 4 August 1997, pp. 88–90.

58. This was the caption for Yash's *Dil To Pagal Hai* (*The Heart Is Crazy*, 1997).
59. The first Indian feature film, *Raja Harishchandra*, had a bathtub sequence. All the women in wet saris were actually men.
60. *Kabhi Kabhie, Chandni, Dil To Pagal Hai* had rain sequences. In *Silsila*, the heroine gets soaked while playing Holi, the festival of colours.
61. Prem in Sooraj Barjatya's *Maine Pyar Kiya* is also partial to leather jackets and motorbikes.
62. A deleted scene shows that Simran is always late.
63. In this scene, actor Anupam Kher used the names of his real-life uncles who were not successful academically. 'They were very happy,' he says.
64. In *Yash Chopra* (London: BFI, 2002, p. 3), Rachel Dwyer writes that many people have remarked how the character is 'so like Yash Chopra'.
65. This shot gave Aditya the idea for Yash's *Dil To Pagal Hai*, in which the lovers don't meet till interval point.
66. In Yash's *Chandni* also, the heroine drinks cognac and passes out.
67. In 2000, Shah Rukh Khan used this line as the title of a film he produced and starred in.
68. Interestingly, a peripheral character in *Silsila* was named Simran.

69. In the long speech Raj makes during the climax of *DDLJ*, he uses almost the same lines: *'Humko koi hak nahin pahunchta ki hum inko dukh pahunchakar apni khushiyon ke mahal khade karen'* (We have no right to hurt them and then erect our palace of happiness).
70. In an interview with *Filmfare* (April 1996, p. 29), Shah Rukh remarked that his marriage was 'straight out of *Dilwale*'. His wife Gauri's parents were 'dead against the marriage'. But he managed to 'patao (please) all her relatives one by one'.
71. In *Kabhi Khushi Kabhie Gham,* Karan Johar used the ritual to stage an elaborate song sequence.
72. The song was never shot because the film was already too long.
73. See Anupama Chandra, 'Talk Shows: Opening New Channels of Conversation', *India Today,* 15 March 1995, pp. 194–96.
74. See Madhu Jain, 'Soap Operas: Beaming in a Revolution', *India Today,* 31 December 1994, pp. 238–41.
75. An *India Today* cover story, titled 'Sex: An Early Awakening', by Vijay Jung Thapa and Sheela Raval (21 September 1998, pp. 50–56), looked at teenage sex. It quoted several studies, which recorded increasing sexual activity among Indian teenagers. It also noted that the Ministry of Health figures for

Maharashtra in 1997 show that girls younger than 15 accounted for 21.7 per cent of all abortions – more than 41,000 – conducted in the state.

76. An *India Today* article by Shefalee Vasudev ('Sex Only Please', 27 May 2002, pp. 52–53) looked at urban women exploring 'relationships restricted to sex'. In it, Simi Chandran, a twenty-seven-year-old Bangalore-based software engineer, says: 'Why do we make such a big deal about sex? If you get it right, it's fun and like chocolate, you want more.'

Credits

DILWALE DULHANIA LE JAYENGE

India	1995
Directed by	Aditya Chopra
Produced by	Yash Chopra
Story and Screenplay	Aditya Chopra
Dialogue	Javed Siddiqui
Additional Dialogue	Aditya Chopra
Title Suggested by	Mrs Kiron Kher
Cinematography	Manmohan Singh
Editing	Keshav Naidu
Art	Sharmishtha Roy
Music	Jatin–Lalit
Lyrics	Anand Bakshi
Production Company	Yash Raj Films International
Executive Producer	Mahen Vakil

Associate Producers	Pamela Chopra
	Uday Chopra
Production Executive	Rajesh Bhatija
Business Executive	Sahdev Ghei
Chief Accountant	Kanubhai
Accountant	Salim Shaikh
Production Managers	Kundan Pai
	Sanjay Shivalkar
Production Assistant	Deewan Rawat
Office Assistant	Sally Fernandes
Office Boys	Justus
	Peter
	Dutta
	Dinesh
Office Secretary	Balkrishnan Iyer
Chief Assistant Director	Ahmed Siddiqui
Assistants	Karan Johar
	Uday Chopra
	Sameer Sharma
Colour Consultants	Bolon
	Pravin Vaidya
Operative Cameraman	Nazir Khan
Camera Assistants	Suhas Shirodkar
	Ratan Soni
Camera Attendants	Jairam
	Sudhir
Chief Electrician	Ismail Shaikh

Electrician Assistant	Babban
Stills	Ratan Bhatia
Stills Assistant	Robert
Special Publicity Stills	Gautam Rajadhyaksha
Special Effects	Prasad Productions P. Ltd
	M.A. Hateek
	S. Azim
Editing Assistant	V.V. Karnik
Art Assistant	Kasam
Costumes	Pamela Chopra
	Manish Malhotra
	Masculine
	Madhav Men's Mode
	Anjasan
	Prachin's
Shah Rukh Khan's Costumes	Karan Johar
Wardrobe	Shashikant Shelar
Chief Make-up Artist	Pandhari Juker
Make-up Man to Shah Rukh Khan	Ravi Indulkar
Make-up Man to Kajol	Vinod Rathod
Make-up Assistant	Kaju
Hairdresser to Kajol	Felsey D'Souza
Hairdresser to Farida Jalal	Farida Khan
Screen Titles	S. Ghalib

Processed at	Film Centre (Mumbai)
Playback Singers	Lata Mangeshkar
	Asha Bhonsle
	Kumar Sanu
	Udit Narayan
	Pamela Chopra
	Abhijeet
	Manpreet Kaur
	Ajay Trivedi
Music Arranged by	Babloo Chakraborty
Songs Recording	Daman Sood
	Western Outdoors Bombay
Soundtrack	*'Ghar aaja'*;
	'Mere khwabon mein';
	'Rukh ja o dil deewane';
	'Zara sa jhoom';
	'Ho gaya hai';
	'Tuje dekha';
	'Mehndi laga ke';
	'O meri zohra'
Choreography	Saroj Khan
	'Rukh ja o dil deewane';
	Farah Khan
Audiography	Anuj Mathur
Sound Assistants	Suresh Solanki
	Ummer Khan

Dubbing at	Gitanjali Dubbing Theatre
	Aradhana Sound Service
Dolby Prints at	Prasad Film Lab
Re-recording	Arun Bose, Prasad
	Recording Studio (Chennai)
Sound Effects	*Synch:*
	Karnail Singh
	Rajendra Gupta
	Sajjan Chaudhary
	Non-synch:
	Ram Kutty
	Sadanand Shetty
Chief Technician	Rajendra Koregaongar
Tax Consultant	Sekhri & Company
Action	Tinu Verma
	Akbar Bakshi
Publicity Designers	Himanshu
	Rahul Nanda
TV and Radio Publicity	Sachin Enterprises
PRO	Gopal Pandey

Cast

Shah Rukh Khan	Raj Malhotra
Kajol	Simran
Amrish Puri	Chaudhry Baldev Singh
Farida Jalal	Lajwanti
Satish Shah	Ajit Singh

Achla Sachdev	Simran's grandmother
Himani Shivpuri	Simran's aunt
Pooja Ruparel	Chhukti
Lalit Tiwari	Simran's uncle
Anupam Kher	Dharam Veer Malhotra
Parmeet Sethi	Kuljeet
Mandira Bedi	Priti
Arjun Sablok and	
Karan Johar	Raj's friends
Anaita Shroff	Sheena
Damyanti Puri	
Hemlata Deepak	
Pallavi Vyas	
Tulika Tripathi	
Rajesh Bhatija	
Shanker Jyer	
Govind	
Mansoor	
Mohit	
Produced at	Filmistan Studios
	Mehboob Studios

189 minutes 36 seconds
Dolby
In Colour
2.35:1 [Panavision]